DISENTANGLING
GENIUS

Unravel the Seven Knots of Frustration so you can Align Desire with Creative Expression

GILL SCOTT

ISBN: 0692318305

ISBN 13: 978-0692318300

Author Academy Elite

CONTENTS

Rhythm brings Relief

        A Humble Exhibition
Appendix

For Julie Warrington,

My friend, and armour-bearer.

Thank you for your incredible patience with *my* disentangling

and your commitment to pray about everything.

I cherish your genuine pleasure in the
prospect of others' liberation

through the expression of my genius.

To the Tangled, I lived and wrote this message for you.

Now is the time for your disclosure and recreation!

*"They are entangled in the land;
the wilderness has shut them in"*

Exodus 14:3

FOREWORD

I remember meeting Gill several years ago. Although I found her European accent interesting, her unique perspective on life was her true distinction. Clearly, she was a deep thinker on a path toward unraveling her own angst.

You'll see in the pages that follow the proof of her pilgrimage. You'll encounter a brilliant plan laid out for all the geniuses in the room. And in case you're wondering about the intelligent person I'm referring to—that would be you.

Gill acknowledges the fact that many of us are tangled up within our own talents. She writes with courage and compassion by helping us see the patterns that exist just beyond the edges of our awareness. Graciously, she also shows us how to disentangle our own genius.

Consume this book and you'll see yourself with greater clarity.

You'll find a friend who shares your common struggles. But thankfully, you'll also meet a guide who's found some serious shortcuts. And last time I checked saving time and money was a good thing.

Enjoy the poetic prose and articulate expressions that follow. I'm grateful for Gill's willingness to be our tour guide through this important topic that plagues so many creatives.

Invite a posture of peace as we untangle ourselves together.

Kary Oberbrunner
CEO of Redeem the Day and Igniting Souls.
Author of *Day Job to Dream Job, The Deeper Path*, and *Your Secret Name*

INTRODUCTION;
FRUSTRATION SNEAKED IN

"We are tumbleweed in the wild expanse of the West"

●

Something black wriggled in the corner and I tentatively pulled back an obscuring layer only to start with alarm as a black strand stretched, tightened and jangled, screwed itself up and then drew up to a height of random zig-zags, threatening, leering and towering above me, crushing and condensing down into a tiny dot, the negative image of an ancient TV in close-down.

I was in a white room and the lines were rearing up again, advancing, shouting at me silently and overwhelming the vista with violent darkening scribble. They tightened again to a horizontal line. I knew it was a matter of seconds before they crashed over the vacuum white expanse again. I fell to the floor petrified, I could not tell the difference between what I was experiencing as being "in the room" and what was the edge of "me". I was falling between confused boundaries of form and space, undefined.

suddenly invaded by black, jangling **ANGRY line**

Scribbling itself furiously across the space

Jumps and recedes again

Into a dot

On an old black and white television screen

Thickens and squeezes out

all white spaces

Dances threateningly

All is blacked out

Recedes and advances

repeatedly

repeatedly

repeatedly

Warring with the whiteness until I wake

Exhausted by the threat

PASSIVITY OR ACKNOWLEDGEMENT?

There's a popular phrase going around that seems both meaningless and self-explanatory at the same time. I hear it in news interviews and political speeches.

"It is what it is", or the variation on that theme, *"We are where we are"*.

Ludicrously obvious, it is true. In fact it is a vital position to come to if any progress is to be made from that particular point or perspective. It is the ability to have self-awareness and insight. Without it we are tumbleweed in the wild expanses of the West, aimless and yearning without knowing why.

This is a 'state of being' that may at one extreme merely upset a train of thought or, ultimately, topple our very sanity.

Did ever the lilies worry about being clothed or the birds concern themselves about their next meal? No, but then they don't have a soul and they don't have a memory! What of those born with a sensitivity that sometimes engulfs and ambushes them from one season or one second to another?

At an early age I realised I was one of those sensitive souls. I can recall sitting on a double-decker bus as a four-year-old child, staring through the rain-spotted window at the reverse lights of the over-taking slow-moving traffic. In the gloom of that dark morning I can remember thinking *"There's an orchestra playing in my head and no one else realises it!"*

Upon one summer shopping outing in East Anglia, England, at the age of ten, I watched an elderly gentleman struggle between the jagged aisle of café chairs with a walking stick, his shopping and a precari-ous cup and saucer. He was knocked into thoughtlessly by a passing customer and sloshed half of his tea out of the cup. My heart went out to him and I wanted to offer to buy him another drink. I doubted my lowly position to offer this and anyway it would have represented a whole week's pocket money, which others might ridicule.

Forever after I regretted not standing up that day to bring back a smile to his face.

So I recognise I have a compassionate heart for strengthening the misunderstood, overlooked or vulnerable. I have a deeply empathic relational approach and a somewhat quirky and abstract take on life.

As a child and student I showed great artistic flair and success. Being dissuaded from a career in art, I took the sensible and traditional choice to go to University to become a registered nurse as I was led to believe that art could never make me a living.

Having wrestled with the lack of expressive freedom both within my childhood home, career, worship community and personal relation-ships I now feel I am able to lay a trail of hope for those who feel similarly constrained.

Colourful in imagery, rich in source inspiration and entirely practical in my approach, I use gifts to inspire and guide the lacklustre, the disen-chanted and excluded. Jostled by childhood bullying, by institutional containment in the secular and spiritual worlds, emotionally bruised by schoolgirl grooming, marital neglect and harshness, the art I have refined is an expression of pain redeemed and a transformation of the mess life hands us.

I have applied this within my professional work as a bedside hospice nurse, as a professional nurse tutor and lecturer, ministry leader and speaker.

Disentangling Genius is a dramatic picture of depth, contrast, texture and hue, a message that we *can* make sense of it all in the way only each individual can.

SEVEN KNOTS OF FRUSTRATION™

There are seven Knots of Frustration defined and unravelled within the main body of the book. I do not claim to see a particularly obvious sequence or inevitability about these but some will certainly be familiar to you and the others are there as warnings. Each one may be re-aligned by a tailor-made solution.

Knot of CONFUSION – disentangled by The Pattern

Knot of HELPLESSNESS – disentangled by The Demonstration

Knot of DISPLACEMENT – disentangled by The Position

Knot of UNSKILFULNESS – disentangled by The Function

Knot of STUNTEDNESS – disentangled by The Stature

Knot of ISOLATION – disentangled by The Interdependence

Knot of MADNESS – disentangled by The Rhythm

FRUSTRATION SNEAKED IN

Here was the fix I was in.

I'll give you one example of its play upon my life. My family had returned from a long distance shopping trip with a special present for my eldest cousin's 21st birthday. It was an expensive teapot of a dinner service he was collecting. As my Mum lifted it from the presentation box, the base simply severed from its body! A fracture line circled the teapot, simply parting company with the base!

There had long been a certain mind-set in my family that went along these lines. *"It always happens to us! If we buy something, we end up taking it back. If we plan a day out, it rains!"* It was incredibly accurate and true. It was so predictive that it had to be true. That was my experience. And yet it grated on me and I told myself that *I* would not have these problems and *I* would not live disappointed.

I had a fundamental resistance to pessimism but I was steeped in it from babyhood. I had high hopes and anticipation. I was a trier and a conscientious child. I enjoyed natural learning through curiosity and avid reading and I thrived on the praise and accolade that my efforts were rewarded with. However there was a darker side to this, a tendency to compare with others and a sense of inadequacy threatened by comparable or better performance by them.

It was years before I recognised that this trail of common experiences illustrated a recurring theme and that Frustration was the byword, even for a life that strove for excellence, purpose, wholeness and integrity.

Despite a sound education, self-direction, opportunities and success in my career I started to realise that this sub theme was a literal warp in the loom of my life. It ran through everything I did and simply would

not be beaten. It was ugly and arbitrary and continually catching and jamming in the machinery of the progress of creative beauty my life was supposed to be!

Eventually brought to a place of utter resignation I stopped. I had finally had what can only be called a thump in the spiritual solar plexus and dropped like a stone, winded and gasping for breath.

For an apparently interminable amount of time I was curled up in a foetal freeze frame. My diaphragm paralysed, eyes wide and frightened, speechless and breathless I slowly recovered from the respiratory arrest. Slowly movements returned, natural and automatic functions were triggered and short shallow breaths stuttered again. I could breathe!

I began to unravel the choked and matted threads of frustration preventing anything of beauty or worth being accomplished at all. I would have to trust my God that nothing is wasted in His economy. I have found this to be true and I would like to help you too, retrieve the raw genius that became snarled in the machinery of your own particular circumstances.

Let's wind it in, looser now and more fitting and comfortable with the purpose or original piece intended. There is great joy and consolation in salvage, renewal, recycling and restoration!

PART 1:
THE TANGLED

FRUSTRATION: OUR NATURAL WARNING SYSTEM!

At the workbench

Feel the frustration and trace the knots

All seven knots!

Call the mess

Shine the light on the problem

Loosen the tangles

Cut your losses

Salvage and rewind

Re-capture and create

Define and interpret

HERE ARE THREE DESPERATELY TANGLED STRANDS.

Barely able to tell which is which and where the ends are, at least let us understand that I started out with three separate strands. They had promise, they were alluring and they were beautifully complementary, tactile and soft.

Nemesis is black, strong and assuring

Daring is red, bold and bright

Recreation is green, refreshing, and rewarding.

Or were

.....these became horribly stretched, chafed and tangled.

Nemesis became a Nightmare

Daring deteriorated into Dithering

Recreation became stifled with Responsibility

I can hardly tell now, which is which. They are all felted and matted into a clump of ugly fibre.

NEMESIS (OUR "JUST DESSERTS"),
COURAGE............... AND PLAY

Years ago I read a wonderful book called *"Dibs: In search of Self"*. It was a touching story by Dibs' clinical psychologist of the unlocking of the soul of an emotionally lost boy who learned to express himself through play.

*"It was as though he was all tied up in knots,
physically as well as emotionally"[1]*

Even for one with an unpromising start such as Dibs, there is within us all an innate potential to be nurtured, first recognised, discovered and developed. We are all born with potential, unlimited curiosity and capacity. Then the "programming" begins. We start out optimistic, impressionable, uncomplicated and playful.

We are introduced to nursery rhymes and fairy stories that, the world over, are re-told and re-read to help children make sense of a paradoxical world. Life, they soon learn, has a light and a dark side, is a mixture of shadow and sun, of good and evil. Fairy tales encourage us to face inevitable confusion, fear and threat.

All in the end is resolved and the story works out "happily ever after" we are assured. But perhaps too quickly we are exposed to disappointment. Too easily we imbibe the adult cynicism around us that life has only a few elusive happy endings to hand out.

Let me try to help you rewind and reclaim the expectation of your early years and combine it with the wisdom of the story *you* have written so far. I believe you can untangle the choked and matted dreams and hopes, combine afresh with the experience of your life and create a stunning piece of work that is a masterpiece of genius liberated and expressed.

How will you find the energy to do this? By knowing that ***it will*** make a difference to you! Maybe you have no clear dream and consequently frustration has no relevance to you. However as soon as a desire starts to grow, it becomes a living entity.

With all the capacity any living thing has to extend and reach and reproduce, desire may also become distorted, obstructed and contained. It may become either a dream or a nightmare.

My own trapped desire for significance was a nightmare.

I forgot how to play.

Despite steeling myself in the face of resistance and neglect, I was terribly insecure. If you would want to know how that position changed and how I found peace with myself and my God even in the face of serial setbacks, then read on.

By the way, God is an integral person in my life who I will refer to in all sincerity as the one who has held me tight whilst also gently easing the taut and straining fibres of my heart. Allow me to make the point up front that I really don't know how I would have learned anything from my story without Him. Least of all would I have grown through it!

Nevertheless you will find principles that are true and powerful whether or not you have a relationship with God as I do. I desire that you may test how effectively they can work for you as they will for a person of faith.

THREAD 1:
THE NIGHTMARE

Here is a vast white expanse. Blank screen. Black dot ⚫

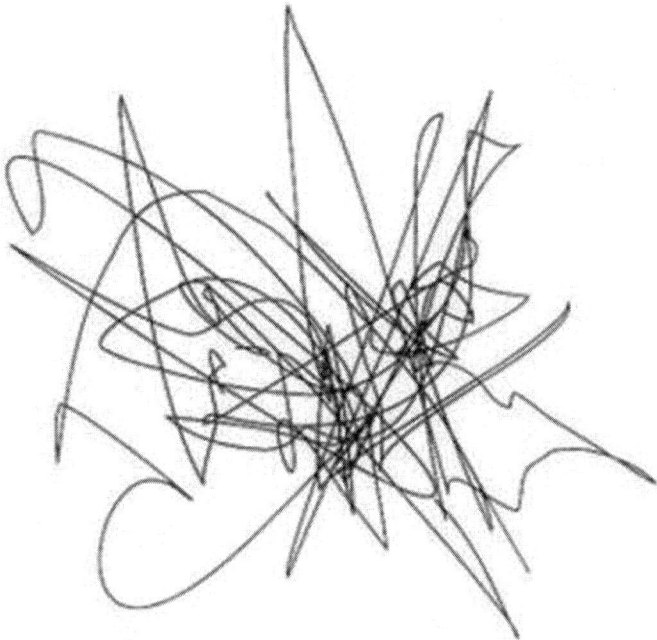

This was my nightmare. This is what it is like to be confused. It is to be shocked, hurting and trembling as a result of fear.

The same reaction is seen in the compelling scenes *No Man's Land* and *Saving the Horse*, of the beautiful 2011 film *The War Horse*[1]. It is a chapter of sheer panic in a gently victorious narrative.

The war horse Joey is alarmed by mortars and an encroaching battle tank until his nerve breaks. He jumps up and clatters over the tank, gallops over and falls into one of the trenches of the Somme then escapes into the ravaged landscape of no man's land. In sheer panic he careers into row after row of spirally wound barbed wire.

At first the speed and determination of his flight is barely interrupted but as the drag of resistance increases, the rough wooden cross pieces flail about his legs. Barbs lacerate and bed into his flesh and he is finally catapulted to an undignified and painful halt. We witness the improbable and poignant collaboration between an English soldier and his opposition.

Braving the war zone to attempt to free Joey, a private realises the situation is futile and Joey is totally caught. A fluently English speaking German joins him to assess the most efficient way of liberating the bound horse. There is a real danger that Joey will worsen his plight once he gains some slack. There must be a simultaneous attempt to cut in a few strategic places.

Enemy troops toss over numerous wire clippers in united and sympathetic armistice, enabling the ensnared victim Joey to be released.

Disentangling Genius similarly and urgently helps those who are subjects, survivors or witnesses of chronic frustration. You may well be your own worst enemy; however, far from this being useful to know, it is disheartening.

I declare that as a seasoned "Frustrated" with a naturally pessimistic outlook there have been times of abject incomprehension and confusion in my life. Only the love of a patient friend and family, sometimes even a complete stranger, the willingness to reflect and grow and an eternal hope in ultimate meaning and salvage has kept me.

I have doggedly picked away at the knots and tangles appearing mysteriously in the results of my carefully ordered intentions! In fact there is no mystery. For some, simply wilful apathy is to blame, worsening self-effort or careless ignorance.

Whether by learning, inspiration or overt correction and support there *is* a pattern to follow. There is a scheme to embellish that will brightly represent everything we *can* be, do and have. This will be in exactly the right medium, circumstances, time, tone and hue.

We are masterpieces waiting to be revealed, untangled or released. As was true for "David", the masterful sculpture by Michelangelo who lay dormant within the marble substance of his confinement, the evidence for and appreciation of our genius then becomes inevitable!

Only its release brings glory to the Master!

Shall we clip and untangle the raw resources within you and boldly re-fashion them into purposeful genius?

INTERFERENCE

My mother had a workbox in which she kept a collection of cotton reels and sewing accessories. She was never really a tailor; however in the sixties it was quite usual for young wives to own a Singer electric sewing machine and learn simple dressmaking skills. Hers had a

black enamelled decorative finish, a thigh operated lever and a wonderful oily metal and workshop aroma that emerged from its arched plywood case. However carefully she would tidy away the reels and various tools it was inexplicably messy the next time she opened the bottle green cardboard accessories box. Miscellaneous pieces of metal rods, attachments and matted threads would be lifted out of the container in a riotous tangle.

She would always comment at the pickle of threads *"Oh the fairies have been at it again!"* I never did find out what most of those tools were for. Nor did Mum progress much farther than making curtains or resorting to mass produced shop garments! The joys of second-hand clothes bargain hunting!

Things just don't stay where you put them! You could say that Mum's sewing box was the earliest exposure to something I would later learn was called the *Law of Entropy of Mass*. I didn't enjoy much about physics at school except for the occasion we witnessed a custard powder tin explosion or the time we caught our breaths as a magnesium floater burned fiercely as it skidded around the water bath in a cascade of brilliant light.

I was a naturally tidy and organised character. This fact of a steady equilibrium of mass in a constantly decaying state of flux from order to disorder really caught my youthful attention.

With much the same impact, the playground jibe *"Get knotted"* used to cause my feelings to smart. Far worse things are heard in school nowadays but it didn't take much to cut me down to size. I was fundamentally averse to the threat of criticism and dismissal.

This was my fear and a recurring nightmare. Incomprehensibly terrifying and confusing, I hated such vehement rejection.

Such potential! Such a spoil!

Ready to be drawn.

Living life as if a genius!

So *"far out"* having nearly fallen over the edge!

Painfully tottering on the edge of genius and insanity?

So heavenly-minded to be no earthly good?

Born *"for such a time as this"* but can't tell the time?

Caught in a mass of barbed wire.

Slowly strangling in No Man's land

Like a panicked war horse breaking rank.

Lost its charge.

THREAD 2:
WE WHO DARE

"dare" verb \'der\:
to have enough courage or confidence to do something
Greek origin, "Tharsus"[1]

By now you have caught the fact that I am convinced of this: We all possess a sense of identity, life and truth that wants to burst out. It is happiest when the rules of common practice are broken.

Sometimes when talking, I forget myself and I become the unfettered girl who played unconsciously or eagerly took up schoolgirl dares. This is who I am and who you are at the core. Whether we ever rediscover him or her depends on how much it matters that we do!

I am calling out to find the frustrated tribe; we know that on the inside we really are free. More free than anyone who is not frustrated or has forgotten what frustrated felt like. Free. Inside.

My passion is for your core freedom to find an exit out from your core into your physical life. If you dare, this freedom will evoke and inspire rather than simply make an impression.

ADJUST AND ADAPT

I grew up in a family of emotional restraint, containment and discipline. As a result of this I became very conscientious, self-directed and somewhat fearful of causing others displeasure. I craved acceptance, spontaneity and adventure and this necessitated a colourful and imaginative inner life. It became my comfort and solace fed by voracious reading and creative writing and journaling.

Solitariness also marked me as someone vulnerable to selfish and demoralising relationships. For three years I was emotionally preoccupied by the focus of a high school teacher whose attentions wreaked havoc with my strong sense of integrity.

I did go on to periodically enjoy a handful of relationships with men who were not particularly secure or mature in their own identity. I consequently nurtured and compensated for them and my "strength" became a rod for my own back. I would endure disappointment in order not to disappoint.

Whilst working very hard in a professional nursing career, I became a mother, church leader and persevering woman in a lacklustre though apparently stable relationship. For seventeen years I was the main provider, advisor and influence within the family. I wrangled over my loneliness and perceived weakness of the man I was with, this father, leader and friend.

As he became increasingly frustrated, insecure and jealous, I found my faith and friendships undermined. There was even doubt cast upon my sexuality and character. I was wilting in this threatening environment of harshness, emotional neglect, mistrust and misunderstanding. I longed to be able to respect and lean on him and felt gagged by my conflicting obligation to respect and "cover" him.

My energies declined, joy was sapped and endeavours in ministry and momentum missed their cue repeatedly. As the Biblical character

Joseph experienced, I felt my *"soul had entered the iron"*[2]. I was depressed and I was dying.

Within a few short years I had already sacrificed a career, experienced loss of ministry and even witnessed the devastating overnight river flooding of the ministry headquarters. My overbalanced sense of identity was toppled and my sanity and integrity scandalised by this relationship.

Fighting a battle of silent resistance I had to hold fast in order that my children and I could become free of the insidious mind games, emotional abuse and personal sabotage. Living from a boxroom and sleeping under a desk for two years, a protracted legal disentanglement ensued.

Relational estrangement was a time of intimacy with God, a sense of His protection and provision and even permission as I realised God loved me even more than the covenant of commitment in such a damaging context.

I slowly unfurled to a new, exacting and privately healing stage of my life. I recognised that recurring patterns of inadequacy, frustration, oversights obscuring my contribution and minimisation of my worth had all gifted me with strong identification with the downtrodden or abandoned.

I carefully identified traits and tendencies that had side-tracked me time after time, repeatedly deferring hope and causing my heart to sicken[3]. I passionately desired to apply reflection and thoughtfulness, curiosity and perceptiveness to help others understand themselves.

Frustration was once the byword for my life and by now I had analysed it so thoroughly I was able to recognise the knotty patterns and tangled interpretations that clouded judgement, obscured potential and strangled my *joie de vivre*.

PERHAPS NOW, IT IS......

Time to unravel.

Time to interpret; time to decipher and decode. Time for you too!

Time to find out what you're really made of and what you're really made for!

Identify the wounds and be healed.

Point to the scars with pride.

Celebrate vulnerability as courage!

Take this as a vantage point as one who is totally winded by the relentless resistance they experienced.

It is time for resilience to be harnessed and not bound!

Time for true genius to be understood and manifested in all its glory!

And so you call Frustration what it is and face it in all its stifling, jeering redundancy.

WE ARE THE TANGLED.

We are the subjects, survivors and thankfully, the supporters or Unpickers of the ravages of disappointment, cold shouldering, obscurity and misrepresentation. We call the mess, the loss and the necessary detours. We cut the losses, we unravel that we may recast, readjust and re-vision.

That's OK. We know now that we have no remaining fear of setback because we have stared it in the face and still stand. We are only the richer for it.

We are those who dare! Where did we get our courage? I can tell you how I came to cultivate mine using the concepts of "*Your Secret Name*"[4], a timely book that started me on this path of disentanglement and liberty. I unwound the string upon string that had wound and tightened me into subjection and immobility over the course of my life.

As name after name had been applied and absorbed into my psyche, this is what I learned about courage. It is not the absence of fear but the determination to get up and fight anyway. But there has to be a reason to get up and fight!

Simply getting up after every knock is not enough in itself. Simply not quitting is not enough. The self- help books don't tell you that! There has to be a higher, compelling vision and it has to be bespoke rather than a flat-pack, pre-cut self-assembly one!

This is my story of daring recovered. Yes I believe we are not born to fear but we learn to fear. Therefore we can recover our innate courage too!

SHE WHO DARED!

I was a sixties baby, the elder of two girls, born at the tail end of the baby boomer years, a new Gen X-er! At the age of five, I experienced great distress one afternoon on the hospital children's ward where I was admitted for tonsillectomy and no one came to visit as expected. I was inconsolable. When I returned to school after a three week convalescence I was acutely ashamed that my peers had learned to tell the time and was intimidated by the teacher's frustration at my complete incomprehension.

At this same school an older girl took to threatening me with her games of Scratch-Tig, scratching my neck every time I was the caught victim. One day at the school canteen she told me I had to stare at the wall without blinking. If I blinked I would die that night at eight p.m. I still couldn't tell the time and went to bed very frightened. Only a nocturnal chat with my Mum put me finally at ease. However nightmares were a frequent occurrence throughout my childhood.

I had a strong group of friends, a vivid imagination and a tendency to get into all sorts of adventures as result of my avid reading of Enid Blyton stories and love of the countryside. This was a cheeky, daring, mischievous, funny and spontaneous child whose sense of exploration was slowly being broken in by a strict and orderly home life and a consequent tendency to retreat into fiction and imagination: the family Bookworm. This was a remedy for long hours in my bedroom for various misadventures such as breakages, lying and experimenting with invented games and improvisations.

When my Mum said no and meted out a punishment, her decision was final and persuasion was pointless. She was the disciplinarian. My Dad's generational awkwardness in showing emotions and being involved in a tactile way started to embarrass me and caused a sense of discomfort about showing my own feelings. Dad's nervous breakdown when I was eight years old was expertly disguised to my sister and me.

Years later we were led to understand that he had moved the family to a new location then resigned from his brand new job at a Further Education College just a few weeks later. Those were lean years with a large mortgage; my mum worked nights in a care home to keep things together. They instilled in me a strong sense of independence and frugality.

MY GIVEN NAMES

Moving school and counties numerous times always seemed exciting but with it came a deep sense of loss and helplessness in being separated from close friends and my familiar neighbourhood. I experienced prolonged settling in periods and a sense of isolation, especially at break times in the schoolyard.

All this contributed to an identity as New Girl, my increasing sense of different-ness exaggerated by my dialect, disrupted relationships and low level teasing. I gained a great deal of comfort in the attentions of my teachers and their delight in my progress with reading, in artistic expression and creative writing. I loved most of my teachers and had crushes on a few of them.

My parents called me the Brainy One (my Sister was known as the Affectionate One). To the teachers I was Star Pupil, Conscientious. One sharp word from anyone would crush me and a strong sense of injustice about others' misreading or interpretation of events would cause me anxiety.

I was investing a great deal of effort in everything I produced and was highly industrious in hobbies and creative pursuits. Occasional flashes of a childlike playfulness would be evident but loud laughter or noise from our sisterly games and rarely visiting friends would be disapproved of from the bottom of the stairs.

By the time I settled into my second high school, I was known at school as Dognose, Swot, Brainbox and at home as Clumsy. Clearly I was not one of the popular or cute girls and high school romance was only an imagined and remote possibility.

At this vulnerable point of my development, a science teacher with a winning and flirtatious appeal evidently noticed my self-containment and attraction, steadily stole my heart and took me on a tortuous journey of deep emotional entanglement. I was investing huge swathes of time in analysing every look and comment and meaning. It wasn't an imagined "grooming"; indeed it was welcomed and savoured but it led only to a major inner battle between heart and mind, between what was possible and what was right.

I was drawn into producing hours' worth of pen and ink drawings for a book he was writing. It was a book that never materialised and for which I never received any reimbursement or recognition. After three years, on a penultimate encounter I resisted overt advances after the 16 year-olds' graduation certificate evening and suffered the rebuff of his frustration as he drove away and sniped *"Go and be a nun then!"*

Inadequacy about my abilities and appeal developed a tendency to inner self-criticism and comparison with others. I was equally hard on myself as a perfectionist focussed on achievement and aspiration. Leaving home at eighteen for University was the most thrilling and liberating chapter of my life, although I did feel badly that I was so ready to move on.

Success came to me on an academic level and a purpose and enjoyment of learning deepened. My Christian faith flowered and I understood the power of fellowship for the first time. Until then my faith had been a very self-directed affair in a traditional and uninspiring church context.

Less successful relationally, I was jilted in two respective year-long relationships. One aborted relationship left me abandoned in Edinburgh, Scotland, to find my own way home. The second boyfriend simply decided he didn't love me. Thankfully a close and family church added value and a deep sense of belonging to my life and introduced me to one of my best lifelong friends whose children I loved and played with as a young adult friend of theirs. They helped heal the ache of being Single.

The first major loss that devastated me was this dear friend's quite surprisingly sudden emigration to the US. A dent was left in the

church and a gaping hole in my own heart. This was the first of a few local churches I invested in heavily emotionally and financially that struggled to break through and become sustainable.

Having settled my commitment to God first and to trust in His timely provision of a husband, I had within three months of my friend's departure, discovered myself to be the focus of an interesting man who pursued me with rapidly developing interest. I could not believe I had found true love and we were married within nine months of meeting. Soon it became clear that I was the Breadwinner and that I would continue to be largely responsible for the household income.

A major blow within two years was the closure of the struggling family church and an inexplicable distrust between my pastors and my new love. Soon I felt that my adult home city since the age of eighteen had lost all its attractions.

I had our first baby and just as my maternity leave came to an end my elderly mother-in-law was delivered to the UK by one of her overbearing siblings with the instructions that it was our turn to host her and would we pick her up from Heathrow?

Suddenly responsible for a baby and an elderly dependent with no idea of its duration, I also returned to work. I was coping with diverse and heavy demands and a need to find more meaningful and better paid work.

With a big promotion and protracted period of commuting and re-location at the age of thirty-one we moved within the north of England from the city of Hull to provincial Doncaster with a two-year-old daughter after five years of marriage. Mother-in-law having stayed for eleven stressful months had shown up the difficulty her son had in protecting or respecting my boundaries. This brought the strain of caring upon our young family.

I felt totally Misunderstood and my career and home-life had little in common. All my sense of value and esteem came from my work so it was especially asphyxiating to find myself scapegoated by the two senior colleagues. They turned bitterly upon me as a result of a report I had naively written as a relative newcomer.

They doubted my motives, they defended themselves and closed ranks toward me, one calling me Ice-Maiden, probably the most hurtful accusation which had ever been levelled at me. With hindsight I had assumed they would welcome my genuine will to reflect impartially. However, I opened a rift that took years to heal and an insecurity that exposed me to ongoing performance anxiety and fear of failure. At home I was told that Christians should not weakly cave in in such a way. There was no comfort there.

A newly forming friendship with another working mum offered me a place where I felt truly understood and appreciated. I was far too needy within my marriage and I had convinced myself that it was my lot to be strong and resolute. This friend became a perceived threat to my relationship and a tide of jealousy was released that seethed and poisoned the relationship between the two families.

Sometimes my man would suggest that if he had not met me and left his church, friends and neighbourhood, he would by now have been a successful engineer in a great job with his own home.

Following another pregnancy, there were tensions underlying these events and our transition to a new church planted in our town. I was emotionally labile, lonely and exhausted. I cried often and without understanding why. Those around me seemed insensitive to these feelings and I was unable to find assistance in counsel or advice because there was no mutual commitment to the process.

A growing and yearning passion for purpose and significance in life partnered with the excitement of a growing contemporary church

soon elevated both of us to leadership and exposure to high calibre teaching and leadership training.

Fuelled by so much vision and possibility I desired to find a way to escape from my career. My heart was elsewhere but the financial demands of the family required me to stay put and I kept striving.

Frustrated became my latest name. Unfortunately a very messy handover, a controlling baton delegation to us as incoming senior Pastors meant that our confidence was sent reeling and our calling tested. "Excommunicated" by the grandparent church leadership, in taking trusted counsel, we started all over again as the church *dare2live*.

The weight of ministry in its major and minor challenges of betrayals and funding rejections, fluctuating numbers and a very small core team continued to take its toll. I was committed to break through and never give up. Quitting was an anathema to me and I could not understand why, despite the high value placed upon perseverance, courage, integrity and excellence, God's favour constantly eluded us.

Earnest prayers and wildly unrealistic ambitions became increasingly desperate. The persona of my partner and ministry pastor was that of a strong man of faith; however, if I ever so much as leaned on him I felt I would lose my balance and fall.

I simply didn't trust or respect him and I realised this was because he was not respect-able. He totally leaned upon me and I felt burdened by this and acutely stressed by the fear of exposure of his incompetence and clumsiness.

Despite leaving my own employment to inject the leadership required from me more continuously, the church did not grow and my health started to suffer. He and I rarely agreed on outlook or approach. I was over-compensating for him, I was insecure in his lead and I suspected he was deeply disappointed himself if only he could admit it.

I could not understand how couples experienced deepening love with the passage of time. I feared failure and I felt trapped.

Then an interruption of the spiralling frustration took place. One summer dawn our church premises and property were ruined by the devastating floods of the worst kind of British summer in June 2007.

We seemed to find a new hope and breathing space through the enforced loss of momentum. For six months we invested our support and identification with other local victims of the flood. In many ways it was one of the most exciting and relevant initiatives of the church's short six-year life.

Receptivity to the gospel and the heart of God in social action was late endorsement of the power of the church to reach the lost in many imaginative ways.

However we were spent, emotionally, financially and physically. He was increasingly withdrawn, antisocial toward my latest good friend and insanely jealous of our friendship. One day he threw down the gauntlet of church leadership for me to pick up and mercifully began earning money again.

Within three months of this supposed "sabbatical" as we called it and a genuine release in my spirit to pick up the leadership, it was all over. I had effectively been set up to fail. He sabotaged the meetings and doubted my motives. I was criticised, abandoned and cold-shouldered. I acknowledged that such a degree of disunity was fatal and that God could not bless the church.

So I took the heart-wrenching decision to resign. Now I had chosen those most abhorred of names, Quitter and Failure. Having sacrificed career, savings and life insurance to fund a major income reduction and re-mortgaging our home, the ministry had to go after all. In one fell swoop I became Unemployed, ex-Pastor and Betrayer. I was crushed and broken.

Within two weeks I became swamped by depression, isolation and grief. I had to find a job now, he told me. I could hardly believe this insensitivity and in an effort to understand his controlling and obsessive monitoring of my movements I found a probable explanation for his behaviour.

I learned it was characteristic of an intractable condition called Narcissistic Personality Disorder. This was both a blow to me as well as a liberation. I sought a temporary separation in a desperate plea to tap into some clear thinking. He spent the night pacing the floor before abandoning the house at one in the morning only to return noisily twenty minutes later. I barely slept, terrified until woken about five a.m. when he flung open the bedroom door and pinned me under the covers, threatening to return early from work when he would take me to see my parents and tell them what kind of woman I was. I deeply feared the impact of my tattered reputation.

What followed was a crazy whirlwind of panicked flight to relative safety as I took the children and escaped to a relative's house in Wales. In a mixture of sheer agitation and unfolding dismay I received a sharp email from a church leader which had a sickeningly strict and judgmental tone. Our separation was not purposeful or constructive, he commented.

Within a week I had relented, knowing that the only way the children would be relatively secure and continuous in school was to return home. The terrific cost was that I had to agree to a separation from my best friend and support. This was a counsellor's advice. Instead, I had to show that I was the wayward repentant.

Invisible yet Conspicuous. That was my imagined identity in the church that had responded to the call from my distraught man. I died a thousand deaths being blanked by people who had known me for years. A strange conviction arose, transgressing the forbidden contact with my best friend. Despite my apparent disobedience something drove me to answer my heart's need for contact and assurance.

On every count I had lost connection with purpose, activity, hope, friends, public, ministry and work. Redundant, I was diagnosed Depressed. My personal counsellor of two years who had clearly seen an escalating pattern of dangerous behaviour in this period had also disappeared without a trace. Perhaps he was too involved, perhaps he had mysteriously died? I was Abandoned.

Now I knew that the awful truth was that I was emotionally and spiritually Abused. I recognised a loveless relationship with a man who could not empathise or care about anything except how he looked and how his needs would be met. I felt a Fool, a Victim and a Disappointment to the team I had developed and the people we had reached. I was Ashamed.

The Biblical character Jacob has a name that means Deceiver. One night he had an amazing encounter with God when he dreamed of and recognised God's Presence[5]. Jacob had always seemed to me to be an uncomfortable choice of character and inspiration for the launch of dare2live church but his story had always been present in and through the various pieces that had come together to lead us this way.

Now I really understood the nature of our imperfection as we had striven and tried and schemed for years to reach the goal that eluded us. I found that only by sacrificing the very thing I thought I was to fight for, could I really know my destiny. I could only know God as Gill and not as Pastor or Leader.

Myself abandoned, I abandoned everything I had fought for and simply lay prostrate, quietly retreating into a narrow boxroom sleeping space under a desk where I found the only safe place to be myself in an otherwise threatening household, the only strategy for coping with estrangement in a shared house. I could not leave because he would not be able to continue the mortgage payments. Similarly he refused to leave throughout a two-year long stand-off.

Joint counselling was advised, an inappropriate approach for me to feel safe. I was offered an initial telephone conversation with one of

his senior pastors who seemed to hear my story of emotional neglect and his harshness. Later, my man told me that my story had been interpreted as making no sense and that they had *"come across this type of thing before."* I suspected that this supposed betrayal was a fabrication. No one there ever contacted me again.

God was very good in giving me a well-paid job working from home, from this same boxroom, as a valued and professional health coach. The income, the team camaraderie and deep empathy with people restored some of my confidence and gave the freedom to attend to the demands of separating.

During the induction for this return to salaried work and nursing again, I was given the name Beautiful one day in a very healing conversation by a highly skilled and respected psychotherapist who led our induction. I accepted it because he was talking about my spirit, my character. There was still hope after all.

I came to a realisation that God loved me far more than the integrity of the relationship I was in; yes, even of the institution of marriage. He cared more for my release and the children's sense of right and wrong than the façade of an intact but strangling marriage. My husband continued to believe against all the evidence that I would come to my senses.

Sometimes he stood at the door of my tiny room fiercely muttering in prayer in a threatening manner, jibing me for my behaviour. I had a doorstop rammed into my side of the door. Other times he would ply me with flowers or turn up unannounced at my new local church or the pastor's office. By now I had turned to a church in my hometown. My family was fractured. My son attended the city church with his father and my daughter chose to stay at home.

Throughout these two difficult years my friends were nervous for my safety, even though the worst that happened was emotional strain and fear and the occasional disappearance or breakage of a valued gift. Finally, he left three weeks after the legal deadline given, without so much as packing a toothbrush or a single family photo. As if none of it had ever meant a thing. That night I wept in sheer relief.

Now I was 45, a Divorcee and a Single Mum. Though life was demanding, financially restrictive and filled with challenges of rebuilding trust and confidence in the parenting of two scandalised and bewildered children, I relished the peacefulness of a home again and the slow restoration of hope, if not passion.

I continued to fight depression and a battle with futility and suicidal thoughts and a sense of isolation from some people who surprisingly preferred to remain impartial. The best outcome of this devastating chapter of my life was a new honesty and love expressed by my parents, a belief in me and a solid trust of my version of events.

Then, following a compounding shock of redundancy five months later, I started to reshape my vulnerable life, launching a coaching business and preparing to complement my now casual and basic income. Once again taking some risks, I invested into a timely partnership opportunity with a certification programme for teaching, coaching and speaking as a John Maxwell Founding Member[6].

Not only did this training add massive value to my healing of identity and sense of significance, it brought me into direct contact with the author of *Your Secret Name*[4], Kary Oberbrunner. He and I recognised a soul connection that stemmed from acknowledged vulnerability through brokenness, the kind he had written about in the book. He gave me a copy and I took away from that Florida conference a key to a new level of healing, intimacy with my Father and a way of seeking purpose and value in the rest of my life.

Reading the book on the return flight to the UK, our plane ascended from Philadelphia, the city named after brotherly love. I was already intrigued by the concept of a Secret Name and I asked God in my heart, "What is my name?" Almost immediately as we rose above the

Delaware, I heard a whisper in my heart that answered the years of intimidation, fear and self-doubt. *"Dares"*.

I sat back in amazement that the very identity of the church dare2live that I had worked so hard to grow, was in fact the projection of an identity God has hidden for me personally!! At a point in my life that circumstances had knocked the confidence I badly needed to recover, this was very timely!

Not only was this something that I secretly hugged to myself as affirmation of stronger days to come, it was a hint at restoration of the mischievousness and adventurousness of my childhood nature.

Not that everything changed overnight; I still had low income, I still found intimacy with God acutely painful and my season of life laborious. Business success didn't unfold as expected and investment was fast outstripping any income.

I knew that there was a yet deeper healing work to be done to the soul wounds I had contracted. For me to dare to be who I was meant to be, there was yet a missing part of that Secret name. Less than a year later I had it.

I always had longed to be pursued, to be brought down from my bedroom from where I was banished, to be chased as a girl, to be loved as we all desire to be. I had despised the fact that I often had to resolve my own problems, couldn't easily lean on or trust significant people.

After being jilted by two boyfriends I had proudly claimed "In future I am not doing the chasing". When I was cut off from my friends and community in the aftermath of my flight to Wales, I was bewildered that my welfare was not sought after by church leaders and anguished that my counsellor had disappeared without explanation.

Here I was considering a pattern of broken and disrupted relationships in my life, either through geographical moves or forced obligation by another party. I realised a clear overall theme of abandonment in my life, a sense of having been orphaned and difficulty in sensing God's love for me. As one who often felt a need for self- reliance yet fantasised about being rescued, I finally realised a name that answered all of this: *"Sought-After"*. And I clearly saw this new name and identity as a seal of my self-worth.

Now I could rise up as *"**Sought-After, Dares**"*. I imagined myself as the five-year-old child who used to love watching Westerns, to dress up and play as a Red Indian, a squaw with a romantic name. Now I could embrace a word spoken clearly into my life a few years earlier as a call to *"Take your stand and declare the full gospel of Christ"*[7].

In fact this was only the start of a new season of unpicking and reworking the stitches of my life. It was a time of new freedom, insights and attention to detail.

Now, my stand or platform is my identity, secure and established and whole.

This story of my wound and its healing is my declaration. Finding my identity as one who dares because she is loved is where I started to get disentangled from all the names, the fears and fantasies.

That's a journey I'd love to take with others who are similarly Tangled. We will go into the studio of your Artist in Residence where the artistry of your own life can be disentangled, defined, revealed and confidently celebrated. Your genius will be found, reclaimed and exalted as the thing that brings most honour and glory to the original Master. You will know your place and purpose in His gallery of masterpieces. All you have to do is to dare to reveal yourself as His workmanship!

THREAD 3:
THE ARTIST IN
RESIDENCE

"It is something to be able to paint a picture, or carve a statue, and to make a few objects beautiful. But it is far more glorious to paint the atmosphere in which we work, to effect the quality of the day. This is the highest of arts." Henry David Thoreau[1]

So how do we go about it?

SUMMER PAINTING SCHOOL

It was a day or two after walking out of my last ever "A" Level examination. I was finally reeling with dizzy relief.

My schooling completely finished, I was riding a bus from Lancaster station to a remote little pottery and studio in the beautiful village of Silverdale, Cumbria. My parents had surprised me with the most wonderful post exam treat. Three solid days at The Wolf House Galleries! I would be one of a random group of delegates attending an outdoor watercolour painting course. I could not have been more excited!

The contrast for me from dusty exam halls and silence to the bird-song, rich bright greenery and shafts of sunlight, the playful easy and recreational atmosphere and home-baked treats served on home-thrown stoneware was a lavish treat to my jaded senses.

Those three days we were taught, challenged and encouraged. We drew and painted outdoors, we were brought mugs of hot choco-late and cookies across the long grassed field. We tried our hands at painting translucent skies, imparting depth as we built the layers of paint and revealed the patches of light. We ate on a first floor mez-zanine patio.

It was perfect, idyllic in every way and a major inspirational boost to the artist in me that was not going to continue with a formal artistic education. Little did I know that in a few weeks I was about to discover I had earned an "A" grade for the Art "A" Level I had just completed. Those three days was such a gift, a really tangible investment of love that I treasured long after.

What if we all had such an opportunity to revel in the space between the activity and the responsibility, between the old and the new, the familiar and the novel? If not in physical retreat at least in a moment, a habit or a discipline that actually became a joy? Memories of that re-freshing time in Silverdale in early summer, 1983, started to play with me and I imagine this is a gift I could pass on to you too!

So here is the third thread as I complete my introduction to the three-stranded cord of genius.

Understandably it is still very tangled but you have seen in chapter one that there is a story, a disposition or a trauma that is The Nightmare, Thread one. For now, we will imagine it is black. The one in my imagi-nation is pitch black, angular and animated!

The Nightmare replaced what should have been our Nemesis! The original meaning of the word Nemesis meant the distributor of fortune, neither good nor bad, simply in due proportion to each according to what was deserved[2].

Interestingly Nemesis was the Greek goddess who dealt justice to Narcissus, who disdained those who loved him. Nemesis was the inescapable agent of his downfall, the one who found him out! We need that retributive quality on a spiritual journey that harbours many agents of frustration to our souls!

Secondly you should have the thread of courage. This courage is needed to face the nightmare and to call the frustrating mess exactly what it is. A total mess. We who dare to do this are the brave. However, more often this thread becomes Dithering rather than Daring, the red of embarrassment or shame rather than boldness and courage. Thread two is supposed to be bright, oxygenated blood-red, taut and strong. Bold and dependable!

Finally, there is your third thread to complete the creative potential we can find. It is a zesty green, peaceful and energising at the same time. It is the green of a fresh early summer leafy bower, a cool and shady hideout from the threat of exposure. Our green strand is looped and soft and tactile. This is the thread of Recreation. However, many become tangled up in Entertainment, an entirely inferior thing.

Why is entertainment so alluring? Because it lulls us into a sense of numbness to the responsibility we ignore. Responsibility overwhelms us rather than recreation refreshing us. I want to help you exchange Nemesis for Nightmare, Daring for Dithering and Recreation for overwhelming Responsibility!

THE STUDIO WITHIN

Let us take up this matted web of colours and come away with it to a place that is spacious, airy and light. This is a place where we can trace and loosen the multiple snarls from the wad of assorted strings. This is a place of concentration and assistance where withdrawal, unpicking and recovery have the patient attention they deserve. This is The Studio where genius emerges and skeins of gorgeous silks are wound and softly piled for the next imaginative adventure.

Now imagine your studio space. I want you to be comfortable and inspired. It has to be a safe place, a timeless place where clocks don't tick and the phone doesn't buzz or ring. You wouldn't notice anyway.

Now you are beyond the niggles of household chores and looming deadlines.

What kind of vantage do you have? Do you see rooftops, woodland, interior decor or seascape perhaps? Do you feel secure in the clutter of pots and paints, plants, tools and heaving bookshelves? Or are you calmed by expanses of white canvas and naturally gleaming honey coloured wood, empty surfaces and neat rows of modelling tools?

What is your craft of choice? What is your metaphor?

Naturally I love to mark paper with colour, mixed multi-media multiplying interest, texture and contrast. Chalk and Biro, pastel and paint verge upon each other adding unexpected effects and inter-relationships. Knitting, crochet, sewing and embroidery are not my real crafts but they work powerfully well for our imaginative experimental retreat as I manipulate these materials in my mind with complete dexterity.

THE OLD MASTER

Who is your Master, mentor and muse? Imagine my Artist in residence. Yours too will guide you in your place of discovery.

They meet you in the studio space where you will retreat, reflect and understand the course you have to take and the inner expertise you have to release. I encourage you now to make a trip there and write about its features and place in it everything you desire to adorn the walls and create the right ambience.

Then, skeins of genius may be drawn from within as you associate this personal recreation with inspiration, revelation and joy! Use the studio sketchpad in the appendix as a repository of impressions and embryonic ideas, trusting that they will merge and form a meaningful conclusion by the time you come to create again.

It is the practice and the exercise that draws out the embedded gift. It is the commitment to discover that raises the gold in the pan of dust and stones. You will come to own a sound and integral picture of your uniqueness and expression if you will come with resolved determination to find a way where there has seemed to be no way.

DEFINING YOUR EXPERTISE

First call it what it is and what it is not. Surrender frustration and the fear of failing to capture anything yet again. It is going to be a three-fold combination of Nemesis, Daring and Recreation!

Let me explain. It has been a very elongated disentangling process for me but my choice to be a nurse took me through this test when about ten years ago I started a slow extrication from nursing as a career.

As an idealistic and demoralised professional in 2002, I became in-volved in a fascinating research study to define the nature of nursing expertise[3]. The Royal College of Nursing wanted to be able to come up with a definition of what the genius of a nurse looked like. I knew there was an indefinable essence of nursing that had called me from a very young age but my actual experience was rather more limited and annoying. I began to admit to myself that I had a love/hate relation-ship with nursing.

Although I loved participation at critical moments of vulnerability in people's lives, much of the day-to-day work was clumsy and weari-some. I felt peripheral to and uncomfortable with the world of routine and bureaucratic control.

It still dogged me that I had turned my back on a far more natural gift of painting and drawing. It was especially galling because I was not sensing anywhere near the accomplishment that I should have enjoyed at this stage in my career for all my concerted effort and perseverance.

I started to look more carefully at why I was still here trying. Would this investigation bring a seal of approval to the course I had taken? I had the three strands in quite a tangle.....I certainly had my night-mare! I showed true courage in persisting professionally and person-ally in the moments and over the years of nursing. But how would I be able to recreate my original expectation of this craft?

Exploring the professional's set of values as expressed through nurse-patient relationships was paramount to my study. In seeking to do this, I wondered what the lead researchers were really looking for.

For me the need to notice and define attributes of expertise immedi-ately threw me into a release of energy and passion about previously unnoticed and potentially insignificant moments. During one of those defining moments with my mentor one day, we recognised something in my daughter's old home-made painting pinned over my desk.

It was an abstract wheel that threw out paint streaks as the paper had revolved around a turntable. It suddenly epitomised the nature of the patient-expert nurse interaction. Without movement of the turntable there would only be a painting of random dots and splashes although the very same painterly actions had taken place.

Movement of the turntable created cohesion, patterning and beauty. It reflected the sensitive engagement of the nurse with the patient, the environment and herself. This spoke to me of either connected or disconnected nursing, relationship or task orientation. The two paintings 'with' and 'without' rotation looked completely different.

The difference was in the heart of the action, the underpinning movement itself and at the moment of creation. It became a motif of artistry as a nurse and the craft of nursing, or as I shall call it here, the genius of nursing.

Convergence of many emerging themes of the project began to bring in me an exciting realisation that for the first time in my whole nursing career I felt I was in harmony with my identity as a nurse. This was nothing short of revelatory.

Previously I had felt at odds with the persona of myself as "nurse". All my experience of institutionalised care, uniformity and stereotyping taught me in the early days of student-hood that I had to leave my personality behind in the changing room: a hole of a place that reeked of sweaty shoes.

A poem I wrote as a staff nurse a few years later implied the separation I felt between "management" and "staff". I was experiencing tensions of socialisation into the expected role. If anyone identified or introduced me as a nurse or called me "student" or "staff" rather than using my name, I prickled with discomfort.

The expressive rather than technical elements of nursing had always been the ones that attracted me to nursing in the first place. In fact I had no idea of the required level and range of technical skill!

Though my competencies developed over the years, the technical ones were much more prone to decay through disuse than the artistic and expressive elements of nursing that grew and developed continually in me. Much of what I was rejecting about nursing were those very things that are now seen to be questionable or even abhorrent about the profession i.e. its routine, ritualism, task- focus and hierarchy.

Increasingly authors are crying out for the humanity and artistry in what nurses do to be recognised!

Interestingly, these elements deepened and responded ever more sensitively with maturity and exposure to my own personal experiences and those of others. I received a compliment from a Community Macmillan nurse who took me with her on a few visits that said to me at the end of the day *"You are a good listener…and that is very important in this job"*. This was my beginning of being *"alongside a patient in pain"*[4] as a hospice nurse.

The fantasy that I always returned to if I felt overwhelmed by the constraints and fears of my work were of becoming an art student. I would take a year on a foundation course to experiment with various media and find the expression that suited me. Art was the alternative career option for me when I chose to become a nurse back at grammar school upper sixth.

I had since always had a secret regret that it had been superseded by what seemed to be the more sensible option at the time. Art was the antithesis of everything I saw as prescriptive and restrictive about nursing…. or was, for in my luxurious reflective examination I began to see that what I could do for or with a patient was indeed as much a creative act as the application of brush to paper. For me there would always remain a tension in that bureaucratic restraint upon true

nursing would cause frustration and even despair of ever making a difference to the world of the patient. Nevertheless one could change the world for one patient!

This is the mark of an artist, to be one who is sensitive enough to recognise the anomalies and idiosyncrasies of life and uniquely respond to it without fear of misunderstanding. So whatever you do and wherever you do it I dare you to ask yourself this question:

"Is it a clear celebration of some genius within?"

Can you at least see the slightest clue to a yearning or obscured conviction that betrays your deepest desire and passion?

We can only work with the materials life hands us and indeed we must. I invite you to the studio within, where miraculous works of salvage, recovery and recreation take place. I urge you to take a look behind this studio door before it is so heaped up with the detritus of suppressed hopes and dreams that you can barely squeeze through. Or perhaps you will decide to stop trying and will close the door to your buried genius forever.

Will *your* resident artist remain a prisoner, a hermit or contemplative? Or shall you risk meeting?

PART 2:
KNOTTED

GETTING AT THE DESIRE WITHIN

Perhaps, as I was, you are very frustrated. I knew what lay beneath but how was I to access it, least of all release it? I needed a guide. I needed to be apprenticed to a Master. I would similarly like to help you as I have been helped. There are geniuses who have lived and those still living who have much they can show us on our pilgrimage to expressive and creative liberty. We can also help each other as the tribe of the Disentangled.

Could you,

at last, or

once more,

have clarity,

feel energy

and inspiration?

I like the way this verse puts it, that we continue to seek expression of all that we were meant to be,

> "(Not in your own strength) for it is God who is all the while effectually at work in you (**energising** and **creating** in you the **power** and **desire**) both to **will** and to **work** for His good pleasure and satisfaction and delight."

Philippians 2.13 Amplified[1]

For too long I was operating in the sheer effort of work and desire without properly accessing His energising, power or right will.

Keep asking...............

Keep asking..............

Keep asking..............

So said Mike, the facilitator of an inspirational workshop[2] one day when I owned the fact that I had lost my original enthusiasm. I admitted, flatly.

> "It's hard to invest again when something you believe in has taken everything you are........................... and failed"

Seeing my consternation and vulnerability these words were a healing reiteration from him and I decided I *would* ask once again.

What are you asking for? Especially knowing it could not fail to be granted?

Yes, go on…write it. Let it mark the page for posterity! It deserves to be recorded!

(And this is the purpose that emerged from *my* desire………

I help subjects and survivors of frustration, disappointment and loss to disentangle their genius into freedom so that they can align desire with expression and release their vital and timely purpose.)

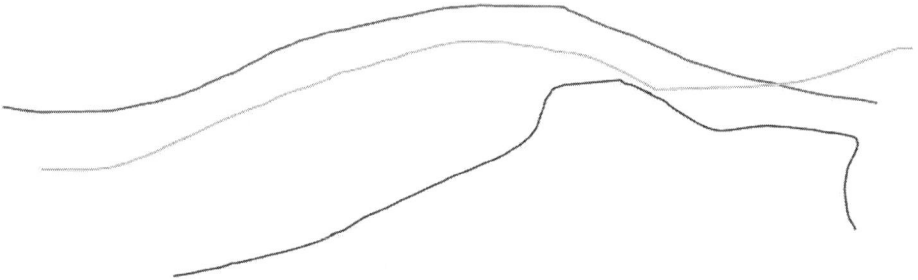

Will *you* dare to disentangle?

To start living AS IF you are all you once believed!

As if you ARE all that you really are!

We will loosen all seven knots of Frustration.

Each one of them represents a **teachable moment** that moves you toward alignment of your desire with its freedom of expression. Take the time you need to extricate each one in the peace of your own studio space.

Your teachable moments are:

1. In CONFUSION, to follow Pattern, co-create and Design......

2. When HELPLESS, to watch the Demonstration..................

3. If DISPLACED..... to Take your stand; find your Position......

4. As UNSKILLED, to ...Function without Frustration............

5. As STUNTED ...to grow to distinctive Stature............

6. When ISOLATED, to interdependently reproduce His Image.

The last, and seventh,

7. MADNESS of repetition ...is relieved by the Rhythm and flow of Genius....

All seven of these actions collectively lead to the real possibility of fulfilment, the alignment of desire with expression!

It is the expression of that which you instinctively know you should be, creatively working out a vital and timely purpose!

Why wait until you have nothing to lose?

Reach the point that you would rather risk failing than regret never having risked!

Do it now while you still have everything to offer!

(At least much more yet than you realise)

Yes,

dare2live!

This is your desire! Whatever the detail, you will add to and embellish it!

Altogether these SEVEN coloured strands represent your Tangled Genius.

Make a careful attempt to intertwine and keep a play of equal tension as you feed all these together into three strands and then one unified coloured cord.

It periodically twists itself into coils, independently and defiantly resisting any teasing on your part to wind it into a ball.

It fails to express creative liberty. You find that something infuriatingly interferes with every repeated attempt you make; every effort to troubleshoot in aligning your desire with expression.

Seven strands interweave to create a central, thick core and a united beautifully attractive cord which we will call Fulfilment or Satisfaction. It is uniquely expressive of our deepest desire!

Unfortunately we often find this is not always our experience. When the knots are snagging, the strands cannot intertwine and combine. Instead of fulfilment you experience the madness of repetition as the cord springs into twisted loops and the soul-destroying task of detour after detour, delay and interruption.

In order to unpick this initial mess of disappointment, I will help you review the condition of your seven coloured strands!

One by one the seven knots of frustration will be unravelled and aligned!

YOUR GUEST GENIUSES

At each of the seven types of knot you encounter, I will introduce to you and your Master, a genius who has already experienced and unpicked one of those seven knots before. They have come to your studio at my invitation to shed light upon your quandary as a result of their own personal disentanglement.

Both the visiting genius and your artist in residence will help you patiently, more confidently and even expertly unravel the seven knots of frustration so that in freedom, you align your desire with its expression! Please, consider what you might want to know of their own first-hand liberation and have ready the questions you want to ask of them. They will linger as long as you need them to!

Each of the seven unintended and contrary knots will be re-tied as an intentional and far more purposeful knot. These knots are the key lesson each genius has to offer you.

There are Seven Genius knots of Pattern, Demonstration, Position, Function, Stature, Interdependence and Rhythm.

So now you can unpick, restore, re-design and re-create your original life as was always intended and perfectly chosen for your unique time and place in the world. Historical and contemporary genius will be your greatest tutor!

DISENTANGLING GENIUS

The Seven Knots of Frustration™

KNOT OF CONFUSION – *"I don't understand what to do"*

Pattern with a Purpose

The original pattern for intended purpose has been scrambled and we feel condemned to repeat to fail or give up in despair.

See the need to stop, examine and get clarity.

KNOT OF HELPLESSNESS – *"I don't know how to do it"*

Demonstration brings definition

We stay ignorant and insecure without trusted and patient examples and natural opportunities to learn, observe and follow Who will be your guide?

KNOT OF DISPLACEMENT – *"I don't know where I belong"*

Reposition for Relevance

Sometimes circumstances conspire against us.

The thing we have to do is to change our context or our perspective of it.

What stance or setting will anchor you?

KNOT OF UNSKILFULNESS – *"I'm no good at this"*

Functionality attracts favour

What you desire is often quietly given away by what you do with ease and flair. Let your talents talk to you!

Do you lack skill?

Where does your passion really lie?

KNOT OF STUNTEDNESS – *"I don't want people to see me"*

Stature makes a statement

Being distinctive draws attention. Sometimes we don't want to risk being noticed.

But we are meant to be noticed!

Do you hesitate with discomfort or courageously display uniqueness?

KNOT OF ISOLATION – *"I can do this myself"*

Interdependence demands integrity

Integration is the most natural and necessary outcome of clearly established position and purpose. Without it we lose our connection with community, meaning and significance.

Who have you chosen to bind to?

What value do you add one another?

KNOT OF MADNESS – *"I've done it all before! Been there, done that, got the T-shirt"*

Rhythm brings relief

We have all heard that the essence of madness is to keep doing the same thing and expect a different result! Genius emerges only as we fail, learn and change accordingly!

What maddening cycle must you stop; what new rhythm will you try?

1. KNOT OF CONFUSION

"I don't understand what to do"

PATTERN WITH A PURPOSE

You sense a universal mission in life to unpick the disorder and tangle of the legacy of your ancient and recent past. You despair over the utterly matted and choked threads of potential.

Sometimes you fight with their incomprehensible resistance and waste them upon secondary functions, poorly matched opportunities and compromises. Other times you abandon potential and inevitably relegate what you once held dear to be the highest intentions over your life. Or, you resign to and accept self-imposed bondage. And sometimes you need to trust the safety restraints that this tangle is allowing you, despite the apparent discord in your life.

I describe the process of Disentangling Genius within a framework, the Seven knots of Frustration.

This is my attempt to draw upon the experiences of restraint I have felt; to describe and illustrate these knotty problems and how to untie them. I will walk closely with you, on behalf of you who may not fully grasp both the amazing potential you carry and sheer vulnerability you risk.

In seeking to undo these knots I know instinctively that it is always better to work into rather than pull away from the tangle, relieving the tension and loosening the mess. I suggest that to lean into your situation which may seem threatening and inexplicable is actually invaluable. You will lean in to slacken this confusion and I will use the slack to loosen and draw out understanding that previously eluded you.

I will introduce the first of our esteemed geniuses to your studio. They are waiting in the "Green Room" (or garden). The really well known geniuses such as Mother Theresa, Nelson Mandela and Martin Luther King were very supportive of the proposal I made them. However, we mutually decided that it would be more beneficial to you, the frustrated, for me to make this invitation to slightly less prominent heroes.

You deserve to experience the power of inspirational examples that have much to teach about the importance of being truly authentic and focussed. Let's meet others who, in getting to the core reason for being, did so whether success was inevitable or not! So I asked a number of my friends who they would want to identify as a *"liberated genius"*. Then I approached a few of their nominations, asking the characters which "knot" their genius particularly identified with.

So first, please welcome Harry Beck[1] who has a tale to tell about overcoming confusion. He signifies our need always to refer to or refine a fundamental pattern.

Here's the KNOT of CONFUSION – *"I don't understand what to do"*

This is OK; confusion is simply a teachable moment! Each one of the knots and invited genius that represent it will give us a teachable moment about that particular frustration and its disentanglement!

When you are confused you need guidance and clarity. So your solution is to **discover a pattern with a purpose!**

Harry Beck drew and refined the London Underground Map. He was a genius at interpreting sprawling opportunities and possibilities into one coherent whole. Nowadays, despite years of obscurity and minimal remuneration, Beck's London Underground Map is recognised as iconic.

DARE TO DREAM

Harry Beck was a London Regional Transport employee with an obsessional spare time occupation that brought to us a design classic and the epitome of graphical clarity in his London Underground map. He was a twenty-nine-year-old engineering draftsman currently laid off work when he deployed his electrical circuitry diagramming skills toward this un-commissioned project.

He set out to represent the underground station network from and for a lay-public perspective. He was determined to impose some kind of sense upon a complex system of 250 miles of track, 273 stations and daily use by 2.5 million passengers. Initially his design was considered "too strange". Harry had realised that he had no need to represent the underground network in relation to its corresponding over-ground landmarks and then he also realised there was no need to show the relative distances between stations to scale. These attachments to realism had actually been a hindrance in producing clear and concise drawings.

His stylised representation boiled down all a passenger would need to know for maximum efficiency in routing their journey with the minimal number of station changes. This also allowed him to disproportionately enlarge the clustered city centre area which de-cluttered the labelling of the most significantly used central area of the network map.

Trialled successfully, loved by the public and yet repeatedly discredited, overlooked and unrewarded by his employers, he continued through trial and error to perfect his diagram, adding the now familiar colour coded lines and achieving in his own mind, a 1949 masterpiece version.

He certainly had a struggle with the resistance of his critics and saboteurs. He didn't understand this and they certainly didn't understand him! He was only once paid a grudging five guineas for his painstaking work. And all the while he was making complete sense of representing the network of the London Underground, making distance travelling accessible for Londoners and the suburban populace. It was a map that would become a template for underground tube travel, subways and Metropolitan lines the world over.

Despite design rejections and resubmissions, the lack of appreciation of his contemporaries, failed attempts by others to enhance his ideas and the disappearance of his name from the ubiquitous posters for decades, Harry's pattern has stood the test of time. Not only that, but it proved adaptive and responsive to growth and changes to the network such as the addition of the Canary Wharf and Docklands extension in the 1990s long after his death.

It has been said of Harry's dedication to improve and refine it, "*touch it in one place and you touch it all over*". The Tube map is a metaphor of our fundamental need for meaningful, interpretable patterns in our lives for direction, orientation and reference.

Let's think of other examples of patterns we encounter in everyday life. Occasionally my mother used to browse through pattern catalogues for the old fashioned tailor's dress patterns that one could buy in the 1970s. Each detailed a picture of the finished article, the recommended fabric and thread for best results.

Inside was a tissue blueprint of pattern pieces that one laid on the material. They were laid either parallel, perpendicular to the selvedge or even diagonally bias cut for a very loose and flowing effect in the finished garment. The instructions made all the difference between success and failure, between a lovely finish or obvious ham-fistedness. Following the guidance dictated the most effective and economical use of the bolt of material and ignoring them was likely to lead to waste.

SENSE SCRAMBLED

Remember, THE original pattern for humanity's intended purpose was scrambled.

No wonder you may have been wandering in confusion!

So you seek to recognise

So you seek to find orientation

So you seek to find understanding

You seek to find a pattern!

Others can comfort, explain or reassure. This is just a start….

When confused, you desire FAMILIARITY/ORIENTATION

………..You follow your pattern and design……………..

Or you retreat into ignorance and panic. (You will never be expected to know what you don't understand. Unfortunately you will have to learn to live with the anxiety).

Confusion deceives and misleads. It triggers a basic and crude reaction rather than a considered response. When we are disorientated we behave in an automatic way and stand to lose the benefit of making

the best of our situation. I have seen this many times in the confusion associated with infection or disorientation in the acutely ill elderly or demented patient. Getting through it is the proverbial Catch 22[2].

FIGHT, FLIGHT OR......?.

The automatic response of living organisms, that one will fight or take flight in a threatening situation, is well documented! When a baby or small mammal is alarmed by a sudden noise, the flight or fight response (a bawl in the case of a baby) is triggered. This can give a momentary state of high acuity to danger, to strategise or at least give an idea to the threatened subject of whether to fight or take flight.

Having learned to compose myself in situations that demand a measured approach, as a nurse under pressure or as a leader with consciousness of my influence and impact upon others, I also recognise that there is a third way. That is to freeze.

Perhaps this third way, understood and used to your benefit, can save you from a wrong and potentially catastrophic decision.

If you fearfully flee, you risk the loss of running from a major benefit you fail to perceive. Or by choosing to fight, you may become harmed by a threat that you are not matched for. What if instead you simply *lean*?

LEAN IN

By doing this you give both yourself and the supposed "aggressor", the benefit of the doubt! Take the example of the elderly man I was once responsible for when I was in charge of a cardiac ward on night duty a couple of years after qualifying as a staff nurse. "Eric" had become disorientated and frightened and failed to understand that the little plastic box looped around his neck with a soft piece of bandage was actually a temporary pacemaker. He fought with me in the corridor of the ward.

His frustration was targeted at the piece of hardware hanging around his neck. It was connected to a subcutaneous wire that directly entered and stimulated the wall of his heart muscle! (Things have progressed since the late 1980s)

It was usual practice to test the treatment plan in this way before a permanent pacemaker was fitted. The external controls were manipulated until a suitable regime was decided upon for the eventual settings of the implanted pacemaker. So, the consultant cardiologist would prescribe the correct frequency and amplitude of the electrical stimulation.

Eric, confused and therefore threatened, was mistaking his "necklace" as a foreign body and he found my approach threatening. I had to shadow him because he had removed the bandage from his neck and all that stood between him and a potentially fatal arrhythmia was my attempt to keep the slack on his vulnerable pacemaker wire!! I leaned toward him to maintain a slightly closer than usual personal space.

My patient all those years ago did not understand that by my holding him and the pacemaker box firmly but closely without tension, I was able to prevent a medical emergency.

DANCING WITH DANGER

So what if instead of fighting or fleeing you simply leaned? You gave both yourself and the supposed aggressor, the benefit of the doubt? Try to lean into the very situation (whatever that means to the context)! This may seem threatening and inexplicable, and it can be invaluable. For example, de-escalation is a technique taught to professionals within any service likely to bring them into contact with frustrated people. It is a technique used especially in anger management. By mirroring the aggressor's tone, then purposefully re-setting a calmer tone, one can bring potentially dangerous emotional amplification back under control. It is more of a dance than a confrontation.

Engaging with the threat rather than running away from it can be instrumental. It may give you the clues you need to defuse the situation and walk away from it without harm. It may enable you to gain new wisdom or even a new friend.

Remember, my appeal to Disentangle Genius is my desire to walk closely on behalf of you who may not have fully grasped the potential and vulnerability you carry. In seeking to undo knots it is always better to work up close, working into rather than pulling away from the tangle, so relieving the tension and loosening the mess.

FREEZE!

So this is what you can you do when you don't know what to do! You can freeze. You can lean into the threat and give it the proximity and concentration it requires to be able to understand the problem it faces you with. You have to recognise that every purpose has a pattern. If the pattern is scrambled, it needs unscrambling so that you can release a potential that is able to be lined up with its purpose. That purpose will be deeply embedded within the gifts and skills and even more fundamentally the core passions and desires of the unique person created for it.

You have a code to break! You have a message to interpret!

We are all born throbbing with purpose and passion to fulfil, with God, His ordained plan in collaboration and creative imagination.

We are all created in the image of God so why is it such a struggle?

That spiritual perfection became *genetically scrambled* in the Garden of Eden.

We may not know it, though we all certainly feel it. Consequently we face a dilemma. We are drawn to become so much more than we seem to be or feel able to be. Yet we seem condemned to frustration; in all of our efforts to fulfil this blueprint.

HIDDEN TREASURE

There is a song that I think Harry would have really identified with. I am told that the most popular song of all time is *Somewhere over the Rainbow*[3]. I believe it. It caught me out once at a most vulnerable moment when I attended a primary school production as a working Mum. Sitting at the back I had barely settled into my dinky plastic seat when the yearning strains of the song were played as a backing to the children's tableau. In case you are only recalling the melody line of the song I'll remind you of the lyrics. I can see Harry is already smiling ruefully at the familiar sentiment.

Somewhere over the rainbow

Skies are blue,

And the dreams that you dare to dream

Really do come true.

These are the words of the frustrated, those who lead lives of quiet desperation, as the American writer Thoreau[4] commented.

These are yearnings that most of us resonate with.

These are the soulful longings of the heart toward an original purpose and even recognition for which we were intended and created!

I had crowded in at the back of the school hall after a day at my role as a nurse. Typically in this season of my life I was managing a crammed diary with senior responsibilities within a clinical and teaching environment. I was being Mum to two young children and co-leading an emerging contemporary community church with my husband. It had had all its own fledgling problems and struggles. Various tests of our leadership mettle and endurance were telling on us and I especially was bending under the load.

Tears prickled my eyes and overflowed down my reddened cheeks. My heart swelled with pain at the sentiments of the song. The performing children were ignorant of its poignancy and this made it all the more cutting. It seemed to emphasise my sheer incredulity at the stalled position we were in. It aggravated the pain of remorseless resistance we encountered and the longing of my heart to realise all the possibilities that remained stubbornly unfulfilled.

It was just a cruel twist that the root word of the phrase *dare to dream* our church name, dare2live was buried in there! It hit me in the chest where I was already emotionally bruised. *"Why, Oh why can't I?"*

Like Dorothy in *"The Wizard of Oz"*[5], I didn't know if I could keep on expecting hope against hope, in the absence of any tangible results. Like Dorothy, I knew my problem. It wasn't for lack of reaching and straining, dreaming or defining that I was unable to "take off"!

Probably like her though, my pain of comparing and waiting and the fantasy of being rescued was not serving me well and I needed a few companions to help me discover that more lay within than beyond! Indeed the problem for the Scarecrow, Tin Man and the Cowardly Lion was in all of them a lack of self-belief and particularly in the one attribute they each desired.

That was Intelligence for the Tin Man, Courage for the Lion and Caring for the Scarecrow. Each of them had failed to realise that they already possessed these qualities. It took a pilgrimage to The Emerald City to discover themselves.

Studio space

Let's take your tangled mess to the place you imagined, the studio of the artist in residence who is skilful and able to discern the possibilities of your gradual disentanglement. For each of these knots or teachable moments at this point in the chapter please turn to the Studio Space pages at the end of this book to reflect, record and doodle. This is the most valuable element of your disentanglement. Patterns will emerge, ideas spring up and you will start to see solutions and explanations that lead to your emerging liberty.

Harry and the artist in residence have been getting to know one another. Both have a mutual respect for the other as an expert in their field. Your artist can assess the material, identify a starting point, draw up a design and patiently show you techniques and sequences that will take you out of your stranglehold of confusion. Harry has a story to tell about how he did just that!

Now I would like you to lean in and look into your confusion from a different stance.

What is the usual source of confusion in your life?

What would it mean for you to take a different stance in order to know what to do?

Have you noticed an evocative song, memory, painting or film and why is it so?

What is it that you desire or dare to dream?

Does it feel as if this is beyond your reach and what causes you to think so?

Have you placed any value upon it despite your confusion, others' misunderstanding or the ignorance of anyone around you?

Do you have the beginning of what could become a classic design for your life and even others' lives?

What will it take to define, improve and refine it?

What pattern do you recognise that you had never really thought about or realised until now?

What does your pattern or your "yellow brick road" look like?

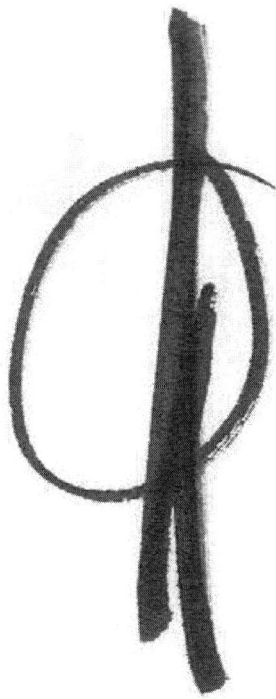

2. KNOT OF HELPLESSNESS

"I don't know how to do it"

DEMONSTRATION BRINGS DEFINITION

The Brothers Grimm re-told an old German tale about an imp-like creature that once stumbled upon a weeping miller's daughter[1].

Her father had told the King that she was able to spin straw into gold. This was in order to look good and impress the King. The poor daughter was at the mercy of this King who threatened her with death if she did not turn all the straw into gold.

I find it odd that the miller did not at least boast that his daughter could grind the straw into gold dust. There might have been half a chance she could intelligently try. But no, he said she could spin straw!! Where would she have ever seen such a thing? The King was piqued, intrigued, maybe even convinced he was going to have a share in this phenomenon!

Thereupon he himself locked up the room, and left her in it alone. So there sat the poor miller's daughter, and for the life of her could not tell what to do, she had no idea how straw could be spun into gold, and she grew more and more frightened, until at last she began to weep.

So entered Rumpelstiltskin.

He was the famed manikin-like creature who seized his moment at her expense. He bargained with her for her necklace in exchange for fulfilling the impossible assignment.

The next day she found herself in an even worse predicament and a larger room full of straw with another death threat to avert. This time the imp extricated a ring in exchange for the task. The third night she was similarly imprisoned and had nothing left of value to bargain with. So the deceitful creature gained a promise from her that she would one day give him her first born in exchange for this third roomful of straw being converted into spun gold.

She knew what was required and what she was supposed to achieve. She lacked know-how, she lacked assistance, a demonstration from the wily creature or even her father. Rumpelstiltskin did not in any way empower her; he simply took over and abused her vulnerability. Now the miller's daughter was beholden to him, rather than the King.

DEMONSTRATION BRINGS DEFINITION

It is tempting when threatened or pressurised with a formidable task, to be lured into a fantasy of rescue or escapism. However there is usually a price for giving away responsibility for solving the problem you have got yourself into.

The miller's daughter recklessly promised her not yet even conceived first-born child.

You are equally in danger of risking your first and foremost reason for being. When you ransom yourself to another who makes sweeping unfounded promises, it is just as disempowering as any original situation you were trying to flee.

That is unless you are genuinely shown a way of escape without terms and conditions! Unless you are able to receive without money or price then you are worsening the knot of helplessness you are already tied with. Without the offer of a simple and genuine demonstration, all trade secrets incorporated, you remain ignorant and insecure. Without trusted, patient examples and natural opportunities to learn, observe and follow you are held ransom to all the unrealistic expectations others or even yourself place upon you.

So who will be your guide? What do you need to be shown?

WINDING BALLS OF NYLON

Often, as a child, I sat on the rough hearth rug of my grandparents' coal-fired dining room of their English northern terrace house. Grandpa patiently untangled and wound the mass of coloured knotted nylon ribbons into individually tight, perfectly formed geometric patterned ostrich egg-shaped balls.

He prided himself on the order and beauty of each creation in his architecturally gifted and skilful hands. I watched the rhythmic movements and simultaneous activity of Grandma knitting the combined threads into brightly striped coat-hanger covers

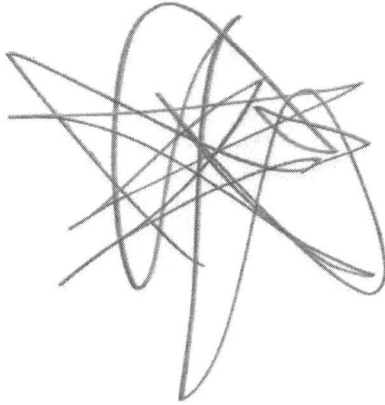

My grandfather had many obscure skills that he prided himself upon. Although a skilled architect by profession I only knew him as a retired pillar of the community and church.

I would help him hand out hymn books on the church steps and tidy them away after the service. He had endless patience and if we visited, would contentedly spend a quiet afternoon peeling and carefully dicing apples, pears and bananas, hulling strawberries and raspberries for a bowl of fruit salad. He sat in his armchair, whipping cream endlessly and hypnotically with a simple fork, or cut bread horizontally, as thinly as wafer ham that one could see the pattern of the plate through!

He taught me how to play Dominoes, Patience and Solitaire and how to build an open coal fire, mount stamps and photographs in his albums and spy on the Rochdale Edenfield Street's Crown Green bowlers with his ancient metallic and tarnished binoculars.

Many years on and a diverse education later I have recognised that I learn most effectively through a demonstration. This is why I loved Domestic Science at school. I comprehended through the combination of theory and practice as the teacher worked and gave a running commentary through all the different cooking methods we had to

master. For me a demonstration was often the difference between information and comprehension. In fact it was essential in novel situations, when my imagination had no precedent to go by!

This was a difficulty I had in understanding a concept until I have been shown an example or technique. However, it gave me an affinity for imaginative teaching techniques, aids, diagrams, analogies and metaphors. No surprises there!

I was a slow learner and that is what probably makes me a sympathetic teacher! This was certainly my battle with Mathematics; there was no picture to focus upon. That was until my cockney math teacher Mrs. Tucker presented me with the visual image she realised I had been projecting in my mind. She exposed the "truth" that I had built myself a wall of resistance, a mental block that I *could not* do maths. Yet there was absolutely no reason why I could not achieve this important leavers' certificate, she said.

It was a revelation to me that she believed I could do it and that I only needed to believe her expert opinion! It was a turning point that altered my aversion to maths and allowed me to gain a decent "B" grade at 16 years of age.

The first knot of frustration we examined, Confusion, was *absolutely not* knowing what to do despite knowing something must be done! Secondly and perhaps even worse than this feeling, is Helplessness, knowing *what* to do, yet not *how* to do it!! They say ignorance is bliss… Well only so long as you stay absolutely ignorant!! Who merely aims for that?

I am ashamed to say that as the aforementioned schoolgirl, burdened by the demands and perceived pressure of revision and exam performance, I used to envy the cows and horses in the fields that I passed on my school bus route every day. They had nothing to worry about other than finding enough grass to eat! They were blissfully, unconsciously incompetent.[2]

Once consciously incompetent, the painful reality of self-doubt starts to kick in and you need a mentor! Oh how you need them!! You need accepting, inspiring mentors and examples. You need learning experiences and safe places to fail.

APPRENTICESHIPS, INTERNS AND MENTORSHIP

Watching, learning and replicating through hands on experience was the concept behind the model of seven years' service apprenticeships arising in the Middle Ages[3]

Whether associated with Universities, Crafts Guilds or Colleges and local government variations of this system have evolved over the centuries. The formalisation and certification of such valuable vocational work based learning was at its height in the 1960's and 1970's until manufacturing in the UK started its demise. It is a model adopted in many professions and informal training programmes, now often called Internships.

The idea that a time-served apprentice could be trained on the job to their optimal level of ability was a pragmatic and attractive one. The levels of expertise became known as craftsman, technician, higher technician, and even graduate. Novices were offered trade specific mentoring, they provided an affordable workforce and guaranteed a supply of emerging tradespeople for the demands of each generation.

Only an apprentice trained as such could become a Master craftsman, therefore a trainer and employer. This was the secret behind early systems of quality and sustainability in manufacturing and trade, long before health and safety legislation and corporate quality management controls.

The KNOT of HELPLESSNESS - sounds like this *"I don't know how to do it"*

Others can show or tell you!

Kids are naturally great at asking for help. Why not reclaim that simple humility in seeking help and advice?

So you seek to find an example

So you seek to find a demonstration

You will stay ignorant and insecure without trusted and patient examples and natural opportunities to learn, observe and follow.

So you seek to find a resource

Who will be your guide?

At this point let me answer the door of your studio to invite in the next guest genius, another Londoner, Michael Faraday. Michael can show you how! He specially wants to contribute whatever he can as an antidote to helplessness. This is his offer of demonstration, a medium he often and expertly used as a science student and later lecturer!

How do *you* learn? Faraday learned by watching and working alongside his mentors and presumably asking many questions!

When you are helpless, you desire an EXAMPLE.

…watch the demonstration, resource your skill…......

DEMONSTRATION BRINGS DEFINITION

Doesn't Michael Faraday look a little out of context in my studio? This is quite an unusual setting for him. However he is more than delighted to assist when he realises that I had approached him because of his wonderful investment as a chemist and physicist.

Probably it is his muted early nineteenth century costume set against the rows of brightly labelled acrylic paints. Usually he is far more at ease in the bowels of the Royal Institution, infused by pungent chemical aromas. The elbows of his shirt are worn and yellowed by stained laboratory benches as he would fiddle with the gas supply of his new Bunsen burner. Shy of adulation or renown, Faraday was a genius science lecturer in the simple explanation of concepts and principles to everyday laypeople and children! He had first heard and taken brilliant notes at a series of the eminent Humphrey Davy's lectures at the age of 21, hankered after a job with Davy and was eventually appointed to be his science assistant.

In the second year of this service, Faraday was privileged to accompany Professor Davy and his wife on a European tour, meeting many influential scientists and later working actively upon Davy and other eminent scientists' experiments. His was the scientific equivalent of a Master's artisan apprenticeship.

As a poorly educated son of a blacksmith he had already served an apprenticeship with a bookbinder for seven years. He had made excellent use of this opportunity to avidly read science books and was already poised for great things at the time of the Industrial Revolution.

The Royal Institution Christmas lectures established by Faraday in 1825 and continuing to this day have become the UK's flagship televised science series. It was certainly obligatory viewing from Boxing Day onward in my own childhood home. As a parentally approved antidote to the excessive Christmas TV diet of *The Morecambe and Wise Show*, *The Many Faces of Mike Yarwood* or endless requests to play the latest game of *Cluedo* or *Mousetrap* we all seemed to enjoy it!.

My Dad was a maths, chemistry and physics teacher himself at this time and owned his own revered copy of Faraday's *The Chemical History of a Candle*[4] I felt as though I was getting a glimpse into Dad's own mysterious world of work in which it seemed he did not make or mend anything of value or bring home tangible hauls from the day's activity.

In fact Faraday and Dad would probably have hit it off as Faraday demonstrated his first primitive discovery of electrolysis or the electro mechanical induction dynamo that first allowed the curiosity of electricity to become a powerful new technology. Dad in return would have reservedly showed him the weird and wonderful elliptical drawing machine he once erected in our front room.

Studio space: *How will you do this?*

What does Faraday have to teach you in particular?

Let's consider what Faraday has provoked in you by coming as a demonstration of his science and his overcoming of the knot of helplessness.

Has he helped you define something that was complicated into something simple and replicable?

Without reading, researching, inviting example and demonstration, your only hope of guiding and showing the way is to pretend infallibility, a precarious and short lived strategy indeed!

You would have to condemn yourself as unteachable or incapable.

Either, you cannot learn or you give up even attempting your task.

Having already understood how important your task is, now failing to follow through with the right method or technique can only lead to one thing!

Frustration…………..! How does that feel?

Could you have been blaming a poverty-stricken or late start in life for your lack of clarity?

How might you learn from Faraday's perseverance through apprenticeships as well as his readiness to capitalise on opportunities that were less obvious?

When you hit a puzzle, dilemma or anomaly, are you curious enough to find answers to the questions on the tip of your tongue?

Faraday was known to be a man of conviction and faith. His strong views were influenced by a branch of the Protestant church called The Sandemanians. They believed in the literal truth of the Bible and tried to recreate the sense of love and community characterising the early Christian Church. This influence was important for Faraday since the theories he developed later in his life were strongly influenced by a belief in a unity of the world.

How might simplicity like Faraday's help you find how to do your thing?

Faraday reputedly rejected both a knighthood and two offers to become President of the Royal Society as well turning down a potential burial in Westminster Abbey. In 1824, he was elected a fellow of the Royal Society at the same time Davy was President. The latter could not see the man who he still thought of as his assistant as becoming a Fellow. Although Davy opposed Faraday's election, he was overruled by the other Fellows. Faraday, nevertheless, continued to hold Davy in the highest regard, never holding the incident against him.

Is it time for you to advance and take even further that which you learned from a master or mentor?

Faraday refused to assist the British government in the production of chemical weapons for use in war. Like him, you may have a point of honour on which you feel challenged.

What principles do you wish to uphold or compromise?

At what cost might this be to your future fulfilment?

One of my favourite preachers often said that he had paid the ticket price for everything he represented. He meant that no one could demand any more from him for the right to tell his own story.

Do you have the right to tell yours?

SO WHAT DEMONSTRATION DO YOU NEED?

I have decided that for me, like Faraday, it means reading and gathering information copiously. Then, I can write, describe, explain and show.

I am passionate about learners having examples and analogies, hands-on experience and learning from practitioners. This is why I resisted the typical path of promotion beyond the realm of competency and stayed in clinical practice as a nurse despite serious and consistent involvement with the academic world, research and education.

I absolutely loved the fact that I might be nursing a dying elderly woman, be engaged in one of her last conversations one evening and be in front of a room full of undergraduate nurses the next morning, fresh with authentic insights, snippets and stories.

Research tradition says that anecdote is the lowest form of credible research. Insights and opinions must be tested and proven.

Educators advocate principles and transferable skills. Now nursing increasingly values expertise arising from intuition and expressed with instinct. Yet at the same time it has tied itself to the scrutiny associated with evidence-based practice and quality performance.

This, for me, was a very messy and confusing bundle of threads to integrate. You too have your equivalent dilemmas to resolve.

So shall we continue unravelling the next of the seven knots?

Now you know HOW to do your thing, you face the next knotty problem of having to place yourself (WHERE) in the correct position to do so. This is beautifully illustrated in the ground-breaking art of an early Renaissance fresco painter. He is waiting impatiently to meet you!

3. KNOT OF DISPLACEMENT

"I don't know where I belong!"

REPOSITION FOR RELEVANCE

I didn't always have clarity. I started out well and visualised great outcomes for my life even as a small child but there wasn't a clear plan.

By the time I was thirty-eight, this desire was jaded and ever beyond my reach. A long overdue holiday in the Baltics was drawing to a close. It was the last evening of our retreat and my husband and I had taken an evening walk along the white beach beyond the strip of pine woodland between it and the cottage we had rented.

It had been an idyllic retreat, in the favoured resort of Lithuania, near Palanga as recommended by Raimonda, a beautiful Lithuanian Doctor I had met professionally a couple of years earlier. Downstairs was rented by a Russian family from Moscow. We stayed in the tropically sticky heat of the upstairs apartment complete with an electric samovar-styled kettle for regular fresh coffees.

We were an intense little family from Doncaster, UK! On this particular night a pall of dread hung over me as we walked barefoot in the sand dunes, through the dusk, for as long as we dared safely leave the sleeping children. I knew that I didn't want to go back home to the life we led. This was more than a sense of the holiday closing down on me. It was a real hangover of the seeming impossibility of everything we were returning to. I took a snapshot of the sinking sun in a pink sky as a backup to the memory I was storing of that rare moment. I had noticed but failed to listen to my heart.

I feel so relieved now, to be on the other side of that ocean of despair. Then, I didn't understand the deceit of false hope. Eleven years later, a print of that photo is still pinned to my office note-board. Another copy is treasured by a friend who walked with me through the lengthy turmoil of disentanglement.

It was only many years and setbacks later before the inevitability of that moment was realised. A year or so on, having related my moment of resistance on the beach to her, I was making plans to travel again. I jokingly gave her the sunset photo. It was a token of my commitment to return in the light of her insecurity about my conviction. On the reverse I had written "I'll be back" but this was more of a half-hearted attempt to convince myself than to put her at ease!

INTERNAL COMFORT; EXTERNAL CONVICTION

Your position has to be comfortable internally before it is convincing externally. Without the inner conviction of one's cause there is a fundamental jarring within the psyche that causes great angst and undermines authenticity. Psychologists call this gap *cognitive dissonance*. I was working very hard to hold the two mismatching truths together in an awkward inner wrestling match that became toxic to my whole being.

For years I did a really good job of projecting a position of strength. Indeed I believed I had one and I believed it to be worthwhile. Inexplicably there was failure after failure to thrive and I always came back to trying harder, picking myself up and starting again, digging deeper for resources and courage.

Or I invested in myself, feeding my spirit and soul. Still my energy waned, my joy dissolved and my expectations evaporated. Perversely I took my lead from the fact that this was all making us more determined, more resistant and was ultimately evidence that we were meant to fight on. *Never give up!* the motivational adage goes. In my case it would have been healthy to do so but we had come too far to give in. (I have only later learned through the helpful writings of Henry Cloud on "Boundaries"[1] and "Necessary Endings"[2] that there is a major difference between letting go and quitting).

REPAIRING STORM DAMAGE

Earlier this year, as I wrote, the network rail line connecting rural Cornwall to the rest of England was re-opened. The great engineer Isambard Kingdom Brunel's Victorian rail-track had suffered devastating damage in the winter storms and lashing waves.

Sagging tracks now hung precariously above a cavernous hole where the sea embankment had collapsed. Teams had worked twenty four hours a day for weeks in foul weather conditions to have this line repaired in time for the Easter holidaymakers.

So when I read the following quote by my hero Watchman Nee[3], the rescued railway story came to mind, illustrating the futility of life at the mercy of instability of conviction. This could have been a description of my own ambivalence about the church *dare2live* I had led.

"Our prayers lay the track down on which God's power can come.

Like a mighty locomotive, His power is irresistible,

but it cannot reach us without rails."

Yes we prayed and worked hard and sought guidance and spiritual strength. The bedrock of conviction was being imperceptibly eroded until one day a major storm took out the very foundation on which these prayers were pinned.

This speaks of the vulnerability of a doubting life and as a woman of faith I certainly take that warning literally. There is a wider implication too about the risk of a poorly maintained inner life. One particular fateful day, catastrophe will suddenly reveal what has been a slow and imperceptible eroding of the inner fabric of character. Lives and assets are threatened so the supply line is cut and what may have seemed to be an utterly remarkable and unshakeable position is called into question. One day you may be a plentiful supply or generous example to family, dependents, friends, clients and populations. Then, suddenly, all of this apparent prosperity has been violently disrupted overnight.

That six week British transport disruption cost the Cornish economy two million pounds a day! What equivalent personal momentum do you risk by overlooking the importance of everyday, mundane responsibilities of life? I include non-emergency prayer, everyday relationship nurture and all those things that are on a par with revision and practice and habit. These unremarkable habits are what enable the power to live advance toward us like a mighty locomotive!

In the classic animated chases between Fred Quimby's cartoon characters Tom and Jerry or in Nick Park's *Wallace and Gromit* adventures it is perfectly possible to lay a track as quickly as the oncoming train is bearing down upon it! In reality this is simply inconceivable!

If we desire to be reliable, weight-carrying, powerful influencers and providers of hope, strength and inspiration to those who come after us, we have to *be ready* and *stay ready* and stable for adversity. Adversity is not the time to lay a foundation! Midnight is not the time to go shopping!

My experience with a shattered ministry proved that strength really does come from weakness. The paradox of failure is that through it, through the very things that one fears, success can come even if it looks nothing like the original vision of success.

Sometimes circumstances do conspire against us in this way. Then we can change our context or our perspective of it.

Speaking with absolute authority on the position or perspective that suffering and containment thrust upon us, Frankl[4] wrote as a prisoner of war. His classic volume on the meaning of suffering wrote about the importance of independence of mind, even within the most awful of situations as not only achievable but liberating. Calling this *"spiritual freedom – which cannot be taken away- that makes life meaningful and purposeful"* he attributed this to be the secret of retaining one's dignity and being worthy of one's sufferings.

Through the majority of my nursing career I too considered this to be an achievable attitude. My patients were people with life-threatening illnesses who were suffering physically and existentially. My attitude liberated me from the crippling inadequacies that practitioners often do feel in the face of death and it also helped me to identify with patients in their apparent powerlessness.

I, too, still choose daily whether the events of life are my master or I am master of them. You also distinguish yourself either by taking a position which is hopeless or still hopeful. We are united as humans with the power of choice between faith and fear. Both are built upon the unknown. Only one is inherently strengthening whatever the outcome.

Sometimes circumstances conspire against you because they don't suit you or you don't suit them! The thing you have to do is to change your context or your perspective of it.

Do you belong? What stance or setting should tether you?

What is your posture?

Will you take a particular stand?

Will you seek to find affinity?

Will you associate with like-minded people?

Will you seek to find the right position?

If not, you will stay where you are, remain uncomfortable and opt to blend and pretend. You understand what to do, how to do it and yet you continue doing it in the wrong context! How relevant is that?

The KNOT of DISPLACEMENT sounds like this: *"I don't know where I belong."*

Once you hear yourself saying this, you can start to discover what you are looking for! You already started this process with the second knot of helplessness! Now for this third knot, to keep seeking what makes sense; what makes you truly secure and fulfilled.

POSITIONING YOUR GENIUS

When you are displaced, you desire an appropriate CONTEXT

.. you find your position, take your stand ...

HOW DO YOU WANT TO POSITION YOURSELF?

My foray into "positional" rather than traditionally ordained ministry began in 2002. It was born out of a failed ministry and a disappointed, retreating leader who personally sabotaged the need to hand over the baton.

Following this rocky sixth month tussle, I received an unmistakeably clear leading from Scripture. I adopted a conviction that we should emerge as *dare2live,* a church to become a tree of great stature. My husband and I considered the inspiring metaphor of the Giant Sequoia trees of the Californian Redwood as our future destiny, even though we were just a sapling tree planted out of tense conflict. We were the tip of a tree that became cut off and re-planted on a hill. This tree grew right at the edge of respectability, the edge of reason, the end of ourselves!

> *I myself will take a shoot from the very top of a cedar and plant it; I will break off a tender sprig from its topmost shoots and plant it on a high and lofty mountain. On the mountain heights of Israel I will plant it; it will produce branches and bear fruit and become a splendid cedar. Birds of every kind will nest in it; they will find shelter in the shade of its branches. All the trees of the field will know that I the LORD bring down the tall tree and make the low tree grow tall. I dry up the green tree and make the dry tree flourish. "`I the LORD have spoken, and I will do it.'" Ez 17: 22-24*[5]

This passage speaks of seven things that characterise the growth of a tree. They are its origin, resource, position, function, stature, interdependence and attraction.

Elsewhere, I call this the *Flow of Fruition*[6] but these same principles apply to our knottily tangled lives. We need a pattern to follow, an example to copy, the correct context, skill at what we do, exponential growth with our interwoven relationships and a life that ultimately attracts everything it naturally needs and personifies. This sequence is followed through every new life, every new career. Like the sap within a tree trunk, it represents a pattern of upwardly cyclical spiralling growth.

I had a fundamental flaw in my pattern. It was a misgiving, an inability to be sure, to see through the conflict and attain all we believed for.

There were deeply considered values I originally stood for and adopted for the church *dare2live.* We were a Daring Alliance for Relevance and Empowerment in life. We upheld Integrity, Courage, Authenticity, Love and Excellence. All these are values to which I still bind myself.

By 2008 what I was truly experiencing deep within the melee of all these laudable aspirations were fear, insecurity, bravado, disappointment, impossibility: collectively a pattern for frustration and failure. I resigned from *dare2live,* the church I had co-led for nearly six years and inevitably it closed two short weeks later. My marriage had fatally fractured as trust was exhausted between us.

I spent a further two years estranged from my husband, albeit under one roof, in a dramatic story that is told elsewhere (*She Dares*)[7]. However, it was a feeble, though growing start of a healing process for me. During this period of healing, stabilising and emotional recovery after the demise of ministry and a marriage that had become so unhelpfully enmeshed with each other, at least I had a new job to focus upon.

By day my home office was my Personal Nurse telephone coaching "surgery". I actually slept there too every night on a roll out mattress squeezed under a desk space in a tiny boxroom.

Our induction trainer had warned us about becoming stir crazy in our home based workspace confinement. Could he have imagined anyone spending nearly twenty four hours in such a tight space? For me it was an altogether safe space, a colourful enclave in a grey and depressing atmosphere. In this room I had access to my work, jealously guarded legal documents and personal journals.

Through my virtual employment I enjoyed regular and salaried earning capacity once more. I had a crammed bookshelf, all my favourite music, access to the internet and the world at my fingers, friendship, entertainment, nibbles and a view of my lively street. All of this was a haven and a life belt to me at a time of minimal socialisation, depression and a severely abrupt end to pastoral connections and responsibilities.

I spent over two years coaching patients on the telephone in this style. The caseloads were workplace employees or long-term condition patients from another county in the UK. I was one of a virtual team of homeworkers who spoke with them on the telephone by appointment. We would coach them toward their own health and wellbeing goals using motivational interviewing skills, however lofty or trivial they might seem.

Over and over again in some phraseology or other I would ask them *"What do you want?"* Their answer might be to "lose 28lb" or "give up smoking", "stop buying chocolate" or "come off insulin". We used semi directive coaching techniques to elicit both desires and ambivalence.

I think that those hundreds of days of probing and listening to the desires of my familiar caseload drove home to me that I had not paid careful attention to my own. I certainly had not worked on them to the degree I was expecting these clients to work on theirs. I had been living a life divided by deep ambivalence and never really acknowledged the dichotomy in my heart.

So this was a period of reflection and active exploration. I had stumbled into a combination of intense workday presence "with" my

caseload. I had started attending small business networking and training and attacking self-development as a leadership coach. I also received some personal coaching that unravelled a huge amount of uncertainty about my Unique Selling Proposition or USP.

The more I investigated, the more confused I seemed to become. But the tide did turn and my business *Motive Leadership* was born. It was the drawing out of the first of three main strands to the masterpiece I would eventually define; a very good start to my emergence from entanglement!

My business name hinted at the fact that the right motive is funda-mental to any successful endeavour. Without that, the conviction and the drive to carry it forward would be a hollow sham or self-decep-tion. To my credit I had only conducted myself ambiguously for two weeks more once the eyes of my heart had been opened to see the futility of my efforts up until 2008. Once my position of failure was declared, my stance was of loss adjustment and I knew I would never be the same again.

I was relieved even if ashamed.

So here was my position: I had failed, was shamed, wasted and frus-trated. These things had flattened me. But in doing so, I realised they had broadened my base and they had made an excellent platform for expansion!

The most stable three dimensional shape in geometry is the pyramid. Once I had been a waving, leaning and fragile "reed" blowing in the breeze, like a dune grass rustled by every eddy or wind. Now, I was more like the dune itself, still capable of mobility and fluidity but es-sentially stable, imposing its presence on the skyline and weighty in its position.

Frustration had become the ugly thread throughout my life and it would continue to be so until I asked and truly answered the question

"What do *I* want?" I heard myself asking clients that very question over and over again in the years that followed but as yet, did not understand its centrality. So far I hadn't dared or even thought to ask myself! This was another teachable moment.

STANCE AND PERSPECTIVE

One of my ex-hospice nursing colleagues used to have an amusing expression for someone who has misunderstood an issue. Announced in her broad South Yorkshire dialect she would retort *"Tha's not wrapped up reyt!"* (Interpretation: "You're not wrapped up right!"). How true this had become of me!

I write now from the joyous and privileged position of having done the hard work of identifying my source of strength and satisfaction and conversely, those soul sapping lies and insecurities. I have actually cut my losses, risked and paid the price of setback, detour and repositioning.

My necessary convictions and clarity to take heart and move forward arose from that and the confidence too. If I had enjoyed these then, I would have been successful. However, I doubt I would have understood my success. Rare are the leaders who have the passion and humility to accurately dissect success for the benefit of others!

GENIUS AT REPOSITIONING FOR RELEVANCE

Some of my favourite lessons, vividly taught by an amusing teacher and local artist, Mr. Hartnup, were in "A" level Art. These lessons were highlights during a very intense and trying period of study. Our art teacher was able to bring to life the enthusiasm, character, style and flaws of the artists we studied and Giotto was the first convincing introduction we had.

Here, today I would like you to meet him too. Yes, it's Giotto the early Renaissance artist who really broke ground in his day with regard to this concept of re-positioning. We are going to meet someone who refused to pretend. Giotto managed it. He was quite unique! Usually it is failure that gives us the gift of insight! By no means was Giotto a failure! Once Giotto might have helped me avoid the catastrophic failures in my life. He knew how to correct long held and undisputed misconceptions without even losing momentum!

So I am inviting him to illustrate to you just how important your self-awareness and consciousness are in selecting a chosen stance.

Please welcome Giotto! As an early renaissance Florentine painter, he is now known as one who broke the mould and bridged the gap of representational life-likeness between sculpture and painting of the day[8]. At this time there was a firmly established tradition of Byzantine art that used pictorial representation as an alternative means of communicating story without language. This was important for the populace who were largely illiterate and needed a visual interpretation of their Bible stories.

It had become irrelevant to attempt to compose figures in relationship to each other for any sense of lifelikeness. Sometimes the artist crammed their subject matter into the picture frame, making distortions of size and shape to use the canvas fully in telling each chapter of a story.

As the art historian Gombrich[9] explained, Giotto was able to break the spell of Byzantine conservatism and release the hints of artistic genius *"under the frozen solemnity of a Byzantine Painting"*. The discoveries had been there for a millennium, since the expertise of the Greeks, but somehow the motivation to pursue these principles had become entangled.

Giotto rediscovered the art of creating the illusion of depth on a flat surface. This was something that would become very fashionable centuries later in the art of Trompe-L'oeil. Illusional depiction leaves nothing to interpretation and is intent upon deceiving the beholder. It requires absolute perfection in execution and mastery of perspective in order to trick the eye successfully.

Giotto clearly came to a crisis as a popular and successful artist of his time. He chose to part company with established wisdom and started to paint what he saw, rather than the things he had been taught to represent and faithfully re-create.

One of the strategies that helped him bring these scenes to life was his habit of visualising. Contemporary friars exhorted people to imagine how a scene looked and felt when they listened to sermons about the gospels. What would a pain-wracked woman in labour, exhausted by her night flight to Bethlehem, be feeling and how would she hold herself in the saddle? With great difficulty I am sure!

Giotto was able to project these images onto canvas in much the same way modern film directors tell compelling tales through their very engaging medium. The emotional impact of Giotto's painting upon his audience must have been as great as that I remember on seeing Spielberg's Jurassic Park[10] and a convincingly animated computer simulated dinosaur close up for the first time.

Scenes of velociraptors clattering around the industrial kitchen of the fated theme park, pouncing at and jumping convincingly like rabid dogs toward a ceiling hatch at the fleeing children were exhilarating. There was a public outcry at the film's Parental Guidance rating at the time, and rightly so, as it was a watershed film that transported the spectator into a frighteningly new level of engagement that was considered overwhelming for young children.

What made it possible for Giotto to change his perspective? Not only did he realise that the standard pictures he was creating did not faithfully reproduce the subject matter before him. He then applied an alternative approach to depicting the human form convincingly. There

had already been some understanding shown of perspective in earlier Byzantine paintings.

Suddenly the compositions he produced became lively; forms were solid, human and had depth. His earliest recognition of foreshortening endued his characters with convincing physical presence. Giotto even went as far as to position figures with their back to the viewer, exactly as would happen in a real-life gathering. This was an age of patronage and the immortalisation of merchants in commissioned art through portraiture.

The thought of patrons or subjects becoming anonymous was unheard of. Whether Giotto was being politically provocative or faithfully purist in his attention to reality we do not know but he certainly had the skill to bring Art to a completely new phase of its history.

SHALL WE ASK HIM?

What could be the equivalent re-positioning that just might change your course of history in some way?

What would be your alternative way of seeing? To no longer churn out the same, the possible, the easy or the expected? It is fine to produce such results as long as they are relevant.

Are they? Still relevant? Fulfilling, or frustrating?

Giotto knew that despite the relative fame and fortune he already enjoyed, he could not deny the special ability he had to represent his subjects faithfully. He abandoned tradition, rules of symbolism and cultural expectations. Wonderfully, he enjoyed even more fame and regional popularity. He, rather than his works, became famous in his own right as one of the earliest celebrities of the art world. Prior to this, work was rarely signed and originating artists rarely honoured so much as the work they created or the religious building they honoured.

Studio space: *Where* will you thrive?

How much enthusiasm are *you* going to keep up for the redundant value that you defend so well, yet so inappropriately or without appreciation?

What do you risk by *coming out* with your alternative view or execution of the thing that you do?

What compelling and engaging truth are you denying the world by replicating the old order of things?

What new phase of your art of living is yet to emerge?

Where are your sights really set?

Take some time to watch Giotto, observing his exploitation of light and shade effects and foreshortening.

He will help you to interpret any gap that you are here to bridge in time and space!

As for me,

I

have been

liberated from

intimidation; all knotty

setbacks have been positively

worked at. I am supernaturally gifted

in untangling confusion, chaos, deception

and disorder, hearing from God naturally for myself

and others and imparting wisdom with prophetic clarity. I know

I am called to recover beauty, strike resonance and bring order from
hopelessly

entangled dreams and purpose. I take my stand and declare fully
the whole restoration by

*"disentangling genius from frustration
to creative and expressive liberty"*

This is my position!

So I ask you in turn, what is more valuable: being unmoved by circumstance or open to change? What is the difference between stability and a bondage of loyalty? How about telling the difference between substance that remains through adversity or "ties that bind" long after one should have severed connection?

One could effectively argue either way. It really is down to timing, context, affinity and leading. Do you know of an absolutely essential connection you must make for your life to really count? Or do you know of a separation you must make that is critical for your survival and thriving?

What do you think your most fundamental motive is for all of that which you dream of? What is this motive you never admit to anyone?

What do you really fear? This is probably a clue to what you really want!

Where are you positioned when your genius flows? Even when re-sponsibility and demands bear down threateningly upon your every last move?

What lies behind all your business/busy-ness?

What is your vision of success? Describe it. Can you draw or paint it?

What is the motive for your desire?

What do you really want? All holds barred.

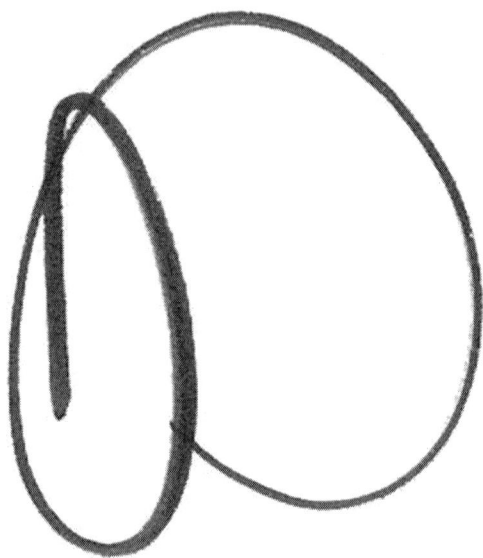

4. KNOT OF UNSKILFULNESS

"I'm no good at this!"

F – U – N – C – T – I – O – N – A –L – I – T – Y ATTRACTS FAVOUR

(Unction[1]. What's yours?)

Well into my forties, I had a tortuous journey of increasingly hopeless attempts to cultivate depth, intimacy and cohesion in a marriage of parallel lives like two parts of a disconnected and unravelling helix.

They had been laid alongside each other, coaxed into position like a child's leaning and top-heavy K'nex[2] construction that could only hold its altitude for so long before the merest change in air pressure breathed a deadly sigh and it collapsed. Only the steadiest hand could possibly have guaranteed its survival to this point of the game. Any reasonable player would have broken it down and stabilised the base first at the early signs of strain. It fell. So completely broken it was, that one would never be able or even want to exactly re-create anything so precarious again.

DYSFUNCTION

Here in my hand were the plastic remnants of a once lofty design. Purple stars and wheels and orange rods were distorted with the force with which they had once been forcibly connected. Stunning and lovely in colour and complementary shape, somehow the scale of the pattern had been misinterpreted in its execution and the pieces had never amounted to a functional model.

In this teachable moment you will learn the need to cultivate and experience heightened competence.

WHEELS AND LOOMS

"Come to our Wacky Women's Group. We're all mad about wool!"

This was an invitation I could hardly refuse! It had come on the back of a conversation with Caroline, an ex-colleague, about my aim of publishing the book *Disentangling Genius*. The metaphor of entanglement is an obvious one and I thought the experience would be a great photo opportunity for knotty images.

Caroline, retired occupational therapist and crafting enthusiast squeezed a spinning wheel into the back of her Honda. Along the country lanes we had a fascinating conversation based upon her detailed knowledge of local history and the proud stubbornness of the ex-mining communities in South Yorkshire.

I had never quite had a day like it. I was welcomed warmly and wandered from spot to spot, spinning wheel to spinning wheel in the Mechanics Institute of Wentworth village. The locally famous benefactors, the Fitzwilliam family funded the village buildings of the Industrial era. This one was now a community hall for diverse groups such as the Spinners, Weavers and Felt-makers! Contrary to Caroline's description there were men and young people present!

In the course of this unusual day I was steeped in conversations about life, purpose, destiny, dreams and frustration. What an amazing opener my writing was! These crafters totally resonated with my book idea and the metaphor of entangled genius!

A psychiatric nurse, Karen, was *"one year and fifty-one weeks"* to retiring and came here occasionally to be grounded and relax, to enjoy the sense of belonging to a tribe and the concurrent productivity of each member during the day. I talked with Karen at length, or rather she talked to me!

As she spun moving her foot rhythmically, feeding her right hand with soft, unbroken yet fragile fibre she prepared the basic one ply thread. Then she showed me a clever Najaro Indian technique for making a three ply interval colour block thread. It was a style of spinning that drew three threads together simultaneously in loop after loop. In fact it was a hand crocheting method.

Karen explained that she always spins for a purpose. She has a gift or a garment in mind that determines and designs the wool created. First, carding or combing would affect the wool's properties. Then the colour, the ply, the thickness of the finishes strand would add their own features to the wool. Then the technical decisions of the spinning methods decided whether to incorporate loose bobbles or cotton strips, mismatching threads to affect the spiral patterning of the thread, additional synthetic glittery threads or whether to spin the wool smooth or loose.

Barbara, another retired occupational therapist spun wool for the sake of spinning wool and only then considered what she might make with it! Mind you she spent most of the time talking and producing very little! Barbara did not identify with the concept of mid-life crisis and the need to return to one's passion to address frustration. This woman had loved and lived every minute of her career, she had never had any sense of distinction between work and play!

I had a hunch that it was possibly more skilful to design and create wool with the end in mind.

"No", Karen disagreed, my it would be equally skilful to make wool as determined by the raw materials and properties of the wool and then only selectively use it when the suitable task or object to make it with came to the fore.

Ruth is the group facilitator and (as I only casually learned), a very influential expert and leader in her field, a world class spinner and international competition adjudicator! Ruth, a trained teacher had from the age of eleven, discovered a flair and passion for spinning, weaving and dyeing. This was offered at "O" and "A" level at her school in Pontefract, the only one in the country to do so. They still were her life's work and play! Now *she epitomised Genius* and I decided she would make an amazing case study of a person living their dream or OPUS[4], loving what they do and doing what they love!! Ruth Gough was Genius Disentangled, aligned, integrated and extremely attractive! The attraction was in her ease, her quiet contentment, authority and evident relationship with everyone.

I had a really powerful insight here. Ruth's experience suggested the path of someone who despite the necessarily hard work of building a business had been "fortunate enough", blessed or lucky, depending upon one's view, to have stumbled across a gift early in life that naturally became an income generating passion! Right from the start of her life she was the existing "designer wool" (such as Karen had crafted) with a purpose in mind and was suited to the task before it was even apparent.

I thought about all the wards I had worked on throughout my nurse training as I sought to discover my niche. As each placement or specialty came to an end I would think to myself *"that's not where I want*

to work" or *"that's not what I want to do".* It had been a matter of trial and error for me and I envied Ruth her early targeting.

Barbara's rather different approach to spinning was to produce wool simply because she had fibre that needed to be spun. Bags of the carded fibre filled up too much space in her home and she worked to condense it into the wool she created. At least until a need became apparent or an opportunity triggered a rummage for just the right-colour and textured skeins she knew she had stored somewhere!.

This was a picture of my life. Industrious? Very! Productive? Yes! Effective? So far, not very effective at all and yet I had a sneaky feeling that the wealth of pre-spun wool and assorted yarns represented my "treasure in the of darkness" a little like Ruth's shed full arrays of rainbow carded wools. My life and yours is an absolutely beautiful article waiting to be crafted and presented when its moment comes!

Karen had said it is just as skilful to create by using the resources in stock, as it was to design with the purpose in mind, The skill was in the choices and combinations of the existing materials rather than the imaginary ones!

Well at nearly fifty years old I am very much an "existing material" rather than potential raw material. Isn't this a powerful and affirming thought to know that all is not wasted and all was not produced in vain? The challenge then for those of us who need to know is not how to "make" but how to "find", disentangle and utilise the overlooked resources in our equivalent context whether it be a box room, a miserable relationship or wool shed!

Ruth had, from the age of eleven, discovered a flair and passion for spinning and weaving. And this was still her life's work and play!

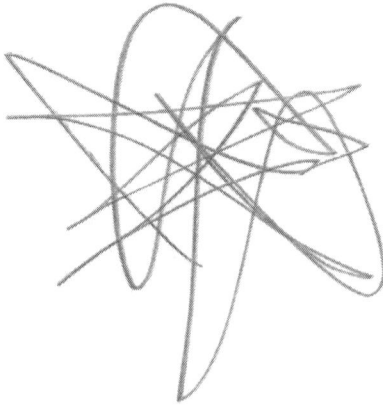

Any parent desires that their offspring's childhood experience is about exposure of unknown potential that lies within. The right context, opportunity, encouragement and belief can find the next Yehudi Menuhin or Jamie Oliver. Being taught to knit, crochet, sew, knock nails and catch caterpillars, press flowers or play in the junior football league are all forays into the unknown possibilities that we might harbour.

You hope that the one thing your children are gifted for will encounter the right opportunity for it to be revealed, early enough to be nurtured and refined to a state of expertise. But how is one accurately able to find out that the child in your charge is a budding Olympic slalom skier or chess mastermind?

KNOT of UNSKILFULNESS - sounds like *"I'm no good at this"*

I did mention Jamie Oliver didn't I? I've made no secret of the fact that I consider Jamie Oliver a real hero. When I deliver training workshops on leadership I confess to the amused delegates that I am a little in love with Jamie Oliver, ten years my junior. He has an enviable track record of success in the kitchen, on TV, in marketing and advertising and campaigning for healthy cooking and eating. His flair demonstrates both productivity and people investment. These are leadership levels 3 and 4 (by John Maxwell's definition[6]). Jamie epitomises the kind of favour and fortune that skilfulness should attract.

As a cheeky, slapdash and entrepreneurial chef with a little bit of preliminary luck he became a UK household name in the 1990s. Jamie didn't leave it there. He capitalised upon publishing opportunities, appeared in many TV series, launched kitchen product ranges, food lines and was especially endeared to our hearts with *"Jamie's Kitchen"*[7], a risky investment into the training and employing of disenfranchised youths within his own catering outlet and eventual chain of restaurants. With the introduction of electronic apps, Jamie was the first chef to capitalise on this medium and the boy (nearly forty now and a multi-millionaire) shows no sign of falling out of favour with the British public.

This Jamie has happily accepted my invitation to the genius party and said he would bring along some pesto and sun dried tomato drizzled potato wedges for Giotto to taste. Only on one condition though, could he bring along his mate Stephen?

You see all this talk about undoing the knot of unskilfulness, for function to bring favour brought home a realisation to Oliver. He had led something of a charmed life. Of course there was always the unwelcome intrusiveness of the press and the strain of growing a young family under the glare of publicity. Yes he had had to put in the "hard yards" at College and chef-ing was particularly challenging socially as a lifestyle. However, there had not been too many sacrifices for Jamie and he had always enjoyed a boatload of confidence!

Stephen would fit the bill for this chapter Jamie suggested. I immediately agreed when he reminded me of this shy and autistic, savant artist. Jamie and Stephen Wiltshire[8] had met some years before at an arts award ceremony he was catering for. It was as if the ease and popularity that Jamie took for granted was wildly contrasted with Stephen's awkwardness with people, his difficulty in stringing together a sentence and all of the celebrity that expertise could have offered him had he wanted or been able to capitalise on it. Here they are now at the door!!

"Let me introduce a top man, Stephen Wiltshire" Jamie announces.

Stephen shifts restlessly from one foot to the other, engrossed in a handful of salted potato wedges. Yet we are all in agreement, he and not Jamie is the one we are fascinated by today. For all his limitations, Wiltshire's genius is well and truly out of the bag. In fact I realise his story also demonstrates the unravelling of the knot of isolation, knot number 6. (I have already invited Thomas Telford to that conversation.)

For now let's just think about Stephen's handle on the 4th knot of function leading to favour.

First, just check that you have a fair assessment of yourself. You may only need a little external assurance and affirmation that you are actually *really* good! That's a fairly easy knot to untangle.

However it could be a bit more awkward than this. Self -belief can be a messy business! True self-belief has to come from the inside.

This is where Stephen Wiltshire helps you so much. He may be shy, awkward and relationally clumsy but he has no doubt whatsoever that he is really excellent at what he does. You may have heard of him. His genius first hit the headlines in 1986 when as an eleven-year-old he was taken in a helicopter over London for a short sightseeing trip.

He was able to faithfully, accurately and intricately illustrate the skyline of the capital to the number of windows and columns, figures and proportionality of the landmarks to one another and every interconnecting road. The general public were flabbergasted.

Stephen simply did what he does best, he drew exactly what he saw in pen and ink on a panoramic poster! He was unfazed by all the excitement about him. He had not overcome many of the psychosocial disabilities he was hindered by. However, his skilfulness in one dramatically unique expression of perspective has guaranteed him a place in the history books and at Jamie's table forever! He has since repeated the remarkable feat of drawing the intricacies of skylines after viewing numerous world cityscapes.

FUNCTIONALITY ATTRACTS FAVOUR

What you really, really want and enjoy is often quietly given away by what you do with ease and flair. I was a keen little artist even as a child and really developed my gifts until my late teens. However the thing I always continued despite time pressures of a family and career was my writing.

I am rarely without a pen! Do you get that insecure feeling when you leave the house, forgetting your phone? I feel that about not having something to write with! It took me a long time to realise writing was my thing and I am confidently owning it now that I do!

Seek to find encouragement

Seek to find wider experience

Seek to find practice opportunities

Seek to find refinement and flair

Otherwise you are agreeing to fulfil the old adage *"Jack of all trades and master of none"*, sticking with low challenge and safety in numbers. You will epitomise "average" and mediocrity which probably won't offend anyone but neither will it attract favour. Again, your choice!!

You can and do excel at SOMETHING! Find it and find favour in it!

When you are unskilled, you desire ENCOURAGEMENT

..become proficient, function without frustration...

What are you good at?

I am no craftswoman, though as a child I tried my hand at Knitting Nancy. Another time I produced an embroidered waistcoat. One grandmother tried to teach me how to crochet. Another had to accept that I was incapable of casting on or off and could merely knit *Dr Who* scarves. In all my childish industriousness and leisure pursuits the pattern was loud and clear! My tool was the pen and much later became the keyboard.

Armed with these is the only time I actually forget to finish a cup of tea!

Only after I had pursued a course of coaching as late as 2012 did I find the definition and clarity for a dream I had for my life. I had already had quite a few nightmares and wild goose chases!

After discovering the OPUS or masterpiece that my life could be through *The Deeper Path*[4], I was extricated from the bewildering confusion that had ensnared me. Previously I had struggled to determine a relevant business proposition. Now I discovered the tell-tale presence of reading, creative writing and journaling throughout my whole life.

I remembered a recent clue. At a business fair showcasing local enterprises, I was blown away when I came upon a young woman's stunning idea to help businesses write their story and distil their signature strength. *Sourcing, defining and writing stories*, that was it! It was something I admired, enjoyed, returned to, embellished in my own journals and had often dabbled in the art of writing a meaningful book.

I had lots of ideas and lots of raw material, false starts and unfinished scripts. The problem was the premise! I didn't have one, nor did I

understand the first thing about target marketing. Unrefined gold it may have been; never mind, this was something I could do! I knew I had discovered a rich seam of direction and resource for my life! This was something I enjoyed and could become totally absorbed in without any sense of time passing. (All these are great clues for discovering one's intended and invaluable Function!)

Do you lack skill?

What you unconsciously desire is often given away by what you do with ease and flair. Let your natural talents talk to you! Where could your passion really lie?

NOW.......

I knit together words that form images of truth and completion.

I write and create inspirational media that can disarm the antagonistic, soften the cold heart and kindle a flame of conviction and joy in the discouraged.

I skilfully lead my reader who may not even know their heart condition to a place of recognition and insight. Writing compelling and unfolding storylines I help people find knowledge, wisdom and understanding.

I facilitate deep calling to deep - creative acts of writing and multimedia that bring glory, honour and expression of a God given artistic authentic purpose.

My insights interpret hidden principles, patterns and precepts.

Through description of experience, imagination and metaphor I enable others to recognise and express their own deeply felt yearnings or unexpressed passions.

This brings them into spiritual discovery, freedom, loosening, momentum and growth.

Studio space: *What does your best look like?*

Now over to you.

What does your preoccupation or gifting look like?

What attributes or activities have resulted in favour and recognition in your life?

How and where do you best express yourself?

What is stopping you from doing it regularly?

What purpose, who and when could this function possibly serve?

I am so excited for you and your self-discovery!

Surely one of the worst mistakes a parent can make at Christmas is to buy their child a contemporary mechanical toy and fail to provide the batteries. Frustration rears its ugly thread again! Without a power source, the toy is redundant and the child is disappointed.

Unction is an old fashioned Pentecostal word that means "to be endued with grace and favour"[1]. It is a special kind of "anointing" that marks one out as set apart, as different and outstanding. This concept of indwelling power for almost unconscious competence also leads us to the next teachable moment about distinctiveness in our next chapter about the fifth knot of frustration.

But just stay with this a moment more! What could your special unction be?

5. KNOT OF STUNTEDNESS

"I don't want people to see me!"

STATURE MAKES A STATEMENT

Do you ever hesitate with discomfort or self-consciousness? Or courageously display uniqueness? Remember Ruth the wool expert and entrepreneurial spinner? Being distinctive draws attention. Sometimes you don't want to risk being noticed. But just as you are meant to notice others, you *are* meant to be noticed!

At first I didn't even notice Ruth. The fairly worn looking sixty-something wore a nondescript baggy grey jumper covered with bits of fluff and snips. She busied herself arranging the trestle tables and registration desk and seemed welcoming, if a little flustered.

In the light of what I saw later that day, she had an incredibly low profile on this fortnightly "self-help" Spinners, Weavers and Felt-making day. It drew enthusiasts from as far away as Skipton, each with their own spinning wheel or portable loom. They came to enjoy the collective working atmosphere, simply to work in each other's company!

Now Ruth was certainly not drawing attention to herself! Her stature became evident in her expertise, her confidence and her knowledgeable authority.

Ruth invited Caroline, my host and volunteer worker at Ruth's *Wingham Wool Works*[1], to show me around the factory shop and cottage industry outhouses. We stepped into shed after shed, turned corners and crossed the wool scattered yard. I started to feel in awe of the stunning way in which Ruth had incorporated everything she loved in life into one distinctive statement. She employed a "family" of workers including her son Tom, whose Rastafarian style locks reminded me of the felt I had just witnessed a woman vigorously creating that afternoon!

These remote and understated business premises were an Aladdin's cave of materials and equipment, tools and machinery with names I had never previously encountered. I came away that afternoon with a whole new vocabulary as well as a visual treat of colour and textural sensation.

Here I might buy a miniature cotton spinning set such as Ghandi habitually used, a device called a niddy-noddy for looping spun wool into skeins, baskets, carders and artisan yarn. Racks of higgledy-piggledy clothes-airers were festooned with loops of yarn, examples of wool recipes for specific colour ways and their resultant knitted samplers.

In addition there were hooks, felt hangings and knitted garments, boxed looms and spinning wheels imported from New Zealand and Poland. Ruth had sourced the best suppliers and she also explained that through their online business orders approximately fifty parcels a day were weighed, parcelled, picked up by the Post Office and dispatched internationally.

She stroked the carding machine hopper lovingly and explained that the machine had just been re-fitted with new needles. It had a well lubricated, hopper that fed into the lethal teeth of the machine to pump out soft fluffy swathes of floaty, silky hairy or even harsh fibre, each designated for a particular use. These then, rolled into thick bands or carded batts, were looped, weighed and sold for spinning.

Ruth couldn't resist joining us on my "tour" and took us into the Rainbow shed. Here were tonnes of wools, carded fibres rolled onto half-length carpet-like rolls in row after row after row of blended colours. Another shed housed the natural wool fibres and smelled faintly of sheep. The scoured, rolled and bagged tops were named after and identified by each original breed.

One mixture of wools was aptly named Shetland Humbug by its neutral stripes. Another was Blue-faced Leicester. Each breed produced wool with a characteristic quality and purpose. Ruth understood the art of choosing and combining appropriate colour and tensile strength for the task in hand. Not only this but the ply and tension as a result of the spinning would add further variables to its application! I started to glimpse the depth of Ruth's genius.

Ruth had also been commissioned to produce adornments and pom-pom accessories for garments made with her dyed merino wool tops by the fashion house Sister by Sibling. She had supplied wool for garments on the catwalk at London fashion week and wool tops for fashion houses such as Ralph Lauren and DKNY at the high end of the market as well as the rural wool festivals at the other!

Ruth is an internationally travelled competition adjudicator and expert, hosts regular textile retreat workshops and gives tuition and advice to pilgrims who come on family holidays or intensives. These are conducted in her garden's open sheltered workspace or conservatory. In with the tuition is the choice of holiday cottage accommodation and bed and breakfast! Her husband Alan is also dedicated to the business, be it servicing spinning wheels or managing the office as well as the horticulture!

I joked about her VAT returns. Ruth had mentioned she was tackling these in the next couple of weeks. I could not have been more surprised that she even claimed to enjoy this exercise! One of her friends had recently been asking her what she would do when she retired.

"What would you do when you retire?" Ruth asked in return. Her friend thought a moment and surmised, *"Well I'd probably have a shed in the garden with a spinning wheel and all my wools and crafts arranged around me"*. Her voice trailed off as the impact of her words hit home.

"Exactly!" Ruth retorted, *"What would I do?"* she laughed ironically.

She turned to me to tell me how she had been fortunate enough to have the opportunity study spinning and weaving at school. Having fallen in love with this, she had found her "thing" early and built a life around it. *"It's been thirty-nine years' work but I loved every minute! And the VAT? That's all part of life's rich tapestry!"* she laughed.

As Caroline and I drew out of the car park, we left Ruth in her garden bringing in the guests' dried bed-sheets from the washing line and her husband carding a large order for bagging in the rear shed. I was filled with respect and awe at their integrated life. I had found someone who had overcome the enemy of insignificance and ordinariness.

On the horizon of her sphere of influence she was a tall tree and a landmark to everyone around her. I desire the same and especially for the love of my cause rather than the need for prominence. I fear not having influence or an impact or legacy. I fear being irrelevant, being forgotten or overlooked and I hate being misunderstood.

I admire the authentic Ruths of this world who make a statement simply by being, and comfortable with all the attention this may bring, yet without being in any way fazed by it!

What do you really fear? This could probably be a strong clue to what you really, really want!

Inspired by the words of Marianne Williamson[2] Nelson Mandela incorporated these words at his Presidential inauguration speech in 1994 after twenty-seven years in captivity.

> *"Our deepest fear is not that we are inadequate; our deepest fear is that we are powerful beyond measure. It is our light not our darkness that most frightens us. We ask ourselves who am I to be so brilliant, gorgeous, talented, fabulous? Actually who are we not to be? You are a child of God. Your playing small does not serve the world. There is nothing enlightened about shrinking so that other people won't feel insecure around you, we are meant to shine, as children do. It is not just in some of us, it is in everyone. As we let our light shine, we unconsciously give other people permission to do the same. As we are liberated from our own fears, our presence automatically liberates others."*

Fear is indeed the common saboteur of our potential.

A THREEFOLD CORD CAN NEVER BE BROKEN!

With this kind of urgent permission and the inspirational example of Ruth, I can take the untangled elements of a striving past. Now I am able to integrate and plait together all seven coloured threads, making three untangled strands and one final, strong unified cord. These are my spheres of influence. This is what I call them.

Disentangled Genius (My defining purpose and brand)

The Flow of Fruition (My spiritual source and expression)

Motive Leadership ("*Make sense of your intent*", my business strapline)

Where did the ease and confidence come from for this to be so clear to me after years of floundering?

It stemmed from the fact that I am no longer an imposter! I probably never was, but the conviction I was had crippled me. I no longer believe I might be an imposter. I have a place "at the table". As a Christian this is a powerful assurance and hope as well as a present daily reality:

"I will invite him to approach me, says the LORD, for who would dare to come unless invited?[3]

I have been sought-after. I will dare!

I *have* been invited, how *dare* I refuse?

I take my stand, rise in stature and confidently declare the whole truth of who I am.

Flashes of cyan, magenta and yellow blend in combinations of red, green and blue.

This kaleidoscope of colour dances, spins, weaves and converges into one pure source and destination of brilliant white.

When we are stunted, or haven't grown as we ought to, we desire ASPIRATION

celebrate strength, grow to distinctive stature......

Now what do you sense? Who or what calls you?

How will you distinguish yourself?

How do you create *your* new order?

How will *you* represent a new liberty?

What is *your* expression?

KNOT of STUNTEDNESS - sounds like *"I don't want people to see me"*

I get this kind of awkwardness. Especially as a British citizen!! But is my or your nationality meant to define us? (Americans may think so!). Joking aside, stunted-ness or the perception that one is stunted is simply another knotty yet teachable moment!

Some people are really uncomfortable at the thought of being prominent. Such a view doesn't serve them well. It certainly isn't helpful when others seek to "bring you down a peg or two" to relieve their own insecurity or inferiority. That's what we call the Tall Poppy Syndrome.

Sometimes, and for fear of being one of those poppies, you may choose to play small so you don't offend anyone. That way we all lose out. The small-minded are not stretched, the gifted stay small and the world is a lesser place for you having been contained.

HOWEVER, STATURE MAKES A BOLD STATEMENT.

Stature is meant to be bold! It is not about being provocative or contrary for the sake of it! It has a mission, a message to convey, a message that is purposeful and impacting. It is other-centred, quite distinct from celebrity based upon external opinion.

I recommend you break off at this point to check that the studio is relatively tidy after Jamie and Stephen's visit. Our next visitor is due and she is very particular about order and neatness! OK, she understands this is a creative space but she is from a very different era. At

least let us pick up any crumbs left over from our earlier impromptu picnic before we go on to disentangle the fifth knot.

Here she is! I'm feeling somewhat awed by meeting this giant of re-form, Florence Nightingale. Especially as I was not an easy fit with her career of choice and focus of her energies, the basis of professional nursing today.

Florence achieved a remarkable scope of influence both in her time and upon the course of the nursing profession which still refers to her seminal work and utilises the core principles of her *Notes on Nursing*[4]

Unusually for one who was to become prominent Florence was a young woman of society who renounced her very comfortable posi-tion to enable her to study and become proficient at nursing. She came from an affluent family who owned two estates.

Her mother was a prestigious socialite. *"I could never quite engage with the endless whirl of parties and tedious conversations about dé-cor, crinolines, prospective suitors and dowries,"* Florence now ex-plains. *"It was much more than a fashionable endeavour for me to be employed in philanthropic works,"* she adds, explaining that this was how her interest in nursing developed.

This was when nursing was a profession perceived to be barely a pro-motion above prostitution. Her parents wanting a good marriage and a respectable social position for her refused to give their permission for Florence to be trained. Only after Florence had refused a marriage proposal and worn them down with fourteen years of pursuing her dream did they finally relent. (So she had already untangled her knot of displacement).

Both she and I decided to become a nurse at the age of seventeen. In my case and because of her legacy, it was a straightforward and laud-able career choice. Florence had to be far bolder! It was not about being provocative or contrary for the sake of it! She had a mission, a message to convey, a message that was purposeful and impacting. It was other-centred, quite distinct from celebrity based upon external opinion.

Being distinctive draws attention. Sometimes you don't want to risk being noticed. But you *are* meant to be noticed! Do you hesitate with discomfort or will you courageously display uniqueness?

For this giant of her era, the Crimean war was her defining moment. Barely through a year's training in a German women's hospital which had already taken its toll upon her health, she heard of the appalling conditions of the medical facilities for the soldiers.

Known already by the War Minister Sidney Herbert, she was positioned as a family connection; she was functioning as a newly trained nurse in the sweet spot of her calling and she responded to the honour to oversee a team of thirty-eight nurses in the Scutari military hospital, Turkey.

For four years she revolutionised the disastrous sanitary conditions, ruthlessly pioneered the simple values of cleanliness, good nutrition and an active mind for these injured and languishing soldiers and reduced the death rate at British military bases by two thirds! Crimean fever cut her mission short and she returned home at the age of 38 to a long campaign of advocacy, advising and establishing a nurses training school at St Thomas' Hospital in London, despite poor health and becoming bed bound for the remainder of her life.

There was no fear of being prominent in Florence's mind. Nor was there anxiety due to possible opposition from the guilt that she might have stirred. In fact she actually campaigned against the enforced idleness of young women of her era. Florence could have hidden in luxury simply because of complacency or satisfaction. No one would have thought badly of her for choosing to be a wife, mother and home-maker. It wouldn't have been wrong to do so, just wrong for her! Nor would we ever have known what heights of honour she went on to achieve. *"I never struggled with complacency"*, she admits, *"there was a bigger work to be done"*.

She was rightly aware of her potential and happily exercised it. There was none of the show of humility that some use as a cover for laziness and fear. Neither did she rail against the apparently brief time she had in the field. She was on the military horizon when she was meant to be and her sphere of influence as an educator, reformer, hospital planning and US Civil War field hospital advisor simply enlarged in a timely manner which she could never have anticipated!

Studio space: *How visible are you?*

She is here now perhaps even to prick your conscience. Are you prepared to own the potential within you and give yourself no excuses, whether they look like successes already tick-boxed or dented pride through abject failure?

What do you have to ask her?

Will you….

Seek to learn that you may teach?

Seek to nurture, to nourish and strengthen your core so that you can strengthen others?

Seek to heal rather than be healed?

Seek to be inquisitive so that you may inspire?

Or will you manage inadequacy by seeking smaller horizons, even anonymity? Conversely (and unhealthily) will you even seek flattery, attention or adulation to compensate for your perceived "smallness"?

What would you really like to be known for?

What is it that will rally you to stand head and shoulders above the others?

What would you give up a lifetime of guaranteed comfort to do?

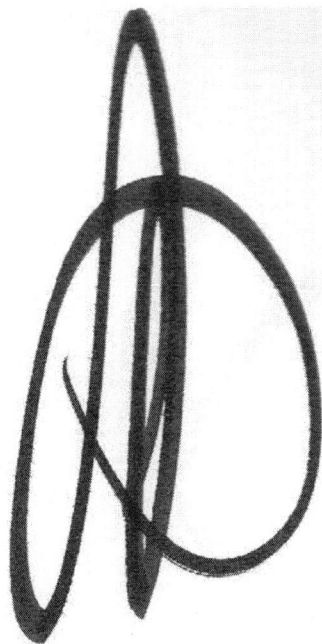

6. KNOT OF ISOLATION

"I can do this myself!"

INTERDEPENDENCE DEMANDS INTEGRITY

Let me remind you of another fairy story of the "Well Loved Tales" Ladybird book series I enjoyed as a child. The story of *"Sleeping Beauty"*[1] lends itself to my next teachable moment about the Frustration knot of isolation.

I am sure that you are familiar with the tale of the King and Queen who desperately longed for a child. One day they were encouraged by a strange speaking frog to expect within the year and upon their baby daughter's birth they threw a christening party for family and friends around. Twelve good fairies from the Kingdom all came to endow magic gifts upon the child.

Only one very old fairy who had never been seen for years was not in-vited. Interesting isn't it, that she had cut herself off for so many years that nobody knew of her whereabouts? She evidently lost out on many such occasions because of her isolation. However this event was on such a national scale that she evidently realised she had been excluded.

Being alone all that time had certainly not been very healthy for her as she gate-crashed the party with a stinking attitude! Vengefully, she declared that the child would prick her finger on a spindle and die at the age of fifteen and then swooped back to her obscure hideout. This thirteenth fairy who had been left out of the loop, ruined the happy occasion with her curse. Horror descended upon the gathering. The twelfth and remaining good fairy who had enough power to soften if not reverse the curse, stepped forward to downgrade the prick of death to a hundred year-long sleep.

Fifteen years later, as prophesied, the King's daughter activated this curse on her very birthday. One day, out of the watchful care of her parents, she found a remote turret of the castle that she had never noticed before. A kingdom wide prohibition and destruction of spinning wheels as a precautionary measure had long been implemented. But this old garret had a spinning wheel secreted away. Indeed this was the wicked fairy's secret location.

Did the inquisitive girl know she should avoid such a thing? Perhaps she had never encountered or heard of a spinning wheel. Or maybe she had been warned and took about as much heed of that as Adam in the Garden of Eden when offered the fruit of the tree of knowledge of good and evil. Whether in ignorance or rebellion, she had stepped outside of her father's protection. Either ignorantly or carelessly, she risked a pricked finger and incurred the curse of a hundred year-long sleep.

What do we see here? That the original ill will toward her was a result of a distorted mind of a disconnected member of society. That on the day her misfortune struck, the king's daughter was out of bounds and apart from the protection of her loving family. Isolation is dangerous. It breeds misfortune, misinterpretation and maybe even misogyny. The saving grace for this girl was that all her family and household fell under the curse along with her. At least they would not all be dead and gone upon her wakening!

We all crave fulfilment, significance and meaning. Something beautiful within each one of us is looking for expression. When there are secrets that we are kept from understanding, our very ignorance can become our downfall; our stealthy curiosity can become a snare. We are meant to learn and grow and have novel experiences *together*, in community and with guidance and support. We are meant to be interdependent, adding value and protection from one generation to another.

Perhaps you have an inner sleeping beauty that is not yet realised, that needs to be awakened and released?

What horror of frustration there would be in thinking that no one else knows of it or seeks it, or values it enough to risk the hedge of thorns that chokes your Palace grounds! What is worse, in fact? Knowing one is a Princess, hostage to terrible frustration or being lulled into a false sense of security and too doped to realise captivity has taken place!!

And how would she ever be wakened? No one knew where she was, no one else in the castle grounds was awake anyway and worse, a thick hedge mysteriously sprang up around the castle making any access impossible.

Some of you sleep too. Deep within, your sleeping genius lies dormant, choked by misconceptions and the curse of generations and knot after knot of frustration.

Everyone we meet has been created to look for and find the reason for living, the meaning of life. Like the young princes from afar, searchers come hoping to awaken a new dimension to life, they hope to receive a possible prize that has been rumoured might be found by others who have gone before them. Then they see the tall hedge of thorns and after a few sharp encounters, vow not to investigate further. Some, more intrepid explorers, excuse your resistance and come tentatively, trying the hedge to see if it will yield, to see if it will let them pass.

How I identify with Sleeping Beauty! So young, so enthusiastic, happy and liberated, all this potential stopped when she ran into the power of the evil that had been spoken against her. She became separated. Everything froze, she was picked off and she was seriously injured. Those who tried to reach her through the hedge of thorns were also seriously injured.

I can also identify with the Princess' suitor. He was attracted to the potential that is surely deep inside, willing to risk the thorns and barbs of the woody twisted and tangled stems, hopeful of a connection that may be life changing.

Little do you know that the moment may have come at the hundred year end when your apparently dense and impassable hedge opens apart, the thorns turn to roses and the foliage swishes quietly behind you as you enter the green tunnel. It barely allows any filtered light through until finally the inside edge of the formidably prickly wall opens and you spill into the brilliant sunshine of the ancient and abandoned courtyard.

I am thankful that someone turned up at just the right time to breach the hedge of thorns around my life. I have learned that we all need each other to release one another's desires. We need each other to bring expression and liberty.

Do you want to be encouraged that you have something worth saying, a painting worth painting or a family worth investing in? Your expression of genius has to have a purpose beyond yourself or there is simply no point in its escaping!

I am thankful that someone glimpsed the genius in me. I am thankful that someone made way for me to glimpse the genius in them. Now I practise the same vulnerability and the same search day in day out to help the slighted, misunderstood, undervalued and the neglected and abused. I disentangle my own unique genius and in so doing, that of others around me.

Those I attract or disentangle are the misunderstood, faltering and obscure. I am drawn to the devalued, oppressed, sabotaged and abused who yet still hope against hope. Those who crave fulfilment, achievement and acknowledgement! The utterly frustrated whose hope has been deferred and whose hearts sicken for expression.

Your sleeping beauty or genius has roused and been awakened by the Prince of all suitors. You also welcome those who follow in his tracks, who come to find out whether they too can gain entrance into your world and you into theirs. Ironically as you become disentangled, you are free to be entangled again by choice, by election rather than default. You align yourself with those you discover. You are similarly being crafted into pattern, design, function, position and stature. Despite what seemed like a hundred-year detour, you now embrace interdependence and only then, ultimately enjoy a beautiful rhythm of life.

Such a "tribe" of aligned individuals bring their respective genius and synergy to communal, purposeful activity so powerfully that everyone is released from sub-optimal performance into engaged, effective artistry. In particular I see these people implement artistic or business flair with empathy and compassion. They bring to life creative, inter-active gifts and talents with combinational power and impact.

Integration is the most natural and necessary outcome of your clearly established position and purpose.

The original meaning of Erasmus' common proverb

"A rolling stone gathers no moss"[2]

has been turned on its head to mean that we should not allow our-selves to be encumbered by responsibility. In fact it was intended to indicate that a frequently replanted plant or tree has little chance of bearing fruit. It appears that the original intent of the proverb saw

the growth of moss as desirable, and that the intent was to condemn mobility as unprofitable. Similarly, we have the Biblical proverb of David

> *"Planted in the house they will flourish!"*[3]

Without such stability and bonding you become disintegrated. You lose your connection with community, meaning, significance and fruitfulness.

Who have you chosen to bind to or run from?

What value do you or could you add to each other?

INTERDEPENDENT ECOLOGY

The giant sequoia is the largest living organism on the whole planet. Yet its roots are disproportionately shallow in relation to its huge stature and profile. In fact its roots could never grow deep enough to support the height and weight of its monstrous trunk. It has to interlink and interweave the roots of other tree systems. Each system uses around an acre of land to become a giant matted platform for stability of the grove.

Could independence of heart be preventing you from relinquishing yourself to that kind of healthy and stabilising enmeshment, a helpful entanglement?

You *have* to be committed to your context in order for your genius to thrive. Shall I say it again, we NEED each other, we work better together and we are more effective when we combine our genii by which I mean genius *plural*. (Is that a word or another fairy-tale character?) Now wouldn't the thought of a personal little genie we could command at every wish be very endearing?

That's not going to happen but the truth that we have to want something badly enough to obtain the power to get it is critical. However, it's not enough simply to desire. It's a starting point but we also need each other.

A business network[4] I once belonged to had a wonderful strapline that stated *"We is better than me"*. Without her Prince the Princess was stuck and so was everyone else in the Palace! Had the curse dictated that the sleeping spell would be broken by a kiss? Nowhere does our classic tale say so, but it was definitely the kiss that did it. This kiss that grew out of wonder and awe brought an end to her dormancy.

This natural and inevitable connection arose from the Prince simply meeting and enjoying the proximity of the renowned Princess. She was released from her tight knot of isolation once and for all!

The Prince was fearless and had vowed the hedge would not restrain him. He knew he had to get through. Of course your commitment to any specific context requires that you too are convinced of your position. (Check again the knot of displacement in chapter 3).

Before you integrate you must first belong. Physically, emotionally, intellectually and spiritually you have to belong before you can begin to believe you have anything to offer or deserve to receive. You have to be convinced of your own and others' value for anyone to stick around long enough to benefit from it!

Do not fall into the trap of remaining isolated out of fear of re-engaging at some risk!

THE COST OF INTEGRATION

Perhaps you still have fears that removing these barriers will expose you to demands you cannot meet. Like Solomon's bride, you are slow to rouse when your lover comes to make demands of your relationship. Perhaps you prefer to be the object of 'his' love rather than the one who loves 'her'. You want your love to be awakened but you don't feel like awakening another's.

Do you know this following extract? It's racy, and worth taking a look!

> I slept but my heart was awake. Listen! My lover is knocking: "Open to me, my sister, my darling, my dove, my flawless one. My head is drenched with dew, my hair with the dampness of the night." I have taken off my robe — must I put it on again? I have washed my feet — must I soil them again? My lover thrust his hand through the latch-opening; my heart began to pound for him. I arose to open for my lover, and my hands dripped with myrrh, my fingers with flowing myrrh, on the handles of the lock. I opened for my lover, but my lover had left; he was gone.[5]

The fairytale Princess Sleeping Beauty was deceived into a deep hundred year-long sleep and Solomon's lover had become complacent in her love of him. Sometimes you too can be similarly lulled into a false sense of security. Despite your professions of desire you become anaesthetised to your original purpose or the call upon your life!

Every thorn can become a blooming rose, every knot, a declaration of genius disentangled! Does someone knock on your door? I assure you they will, but they won't wait forever! Now that your time has come are you delaying a response or pretending to be asleep? How does that serve you or them?

KNOT of ISOLATION – sounds like *"I can do this myself"*

Maybe you can do many things by yourself, but what if others could add their value to what you can do and you could add your value to theirs? Actually I don't think you can do very much yourself. At least

not for very long! Or with any purpose. The severest form of punishment or torture is to be kept in solitary confinement. Isolation does strange things to the psyche!

INTERDEPENDENCE DEMANDS INTEGRITY

Integration is the most natural and necessary outcome of clearly established position and purpose. Without it you lose your connection with community, meaning and significance.

Who have you chosen to bind to?

What value do you add to one another?

John Donne had it right when he said that *"No man is an island"*[6]. One of my favourite films is *"Castaway"*[7], starring Tom Hanks as the executive who disappears for four years after his plane crashes in a tropical storm. You could say he was somewhat frustrated by the turn of events!

His evident need for companionship and accountability is seen when he creates a friend and reference point, Wilson, who is in fact a basketball. Along with a designer dress that becomes a fishing net and an ice skate improvising as a primitive dental implement, Wilson is washed up in a FedEx container. Wilson's purpose is to serve Chuck Noland, Hanks' character, as a vital though imaginary friend.

When we are isolated we......

Seek to find relationship, community and consolation

Seek to find representation, reflection and reproduction

Seek to find integration and interdependence

You and I can more easily predict results that are entirely by our own hand. Remember, "we" *is* better than "me"! Predictable does mean safe and…..predictable!!

So far, six knots out of your tangle, you have realised your lack of comprehension (Confusion), had to find assistance (Helplessness), decided upon a relevant position to take (Displacement) and are becoming skilled at what you do best (leaving behind Unskilfulness).

You have overcome your reticence about becoming larger than life (Stuntedness). Is there any point to all this progress without others to celebrate with (Isolation)? Without others, without connection and relationship you are doomed to extinction or the deception of vanity and self-glorification!

How tragic, let's not stop here, let's keep disentangling!!

When you are independent or isolated, you desire COMMUNITY

…giving and taking, interdependently reproducing One Image..

What can you add to community?

One of my mentors Kary Oberbrunner regularly uses the phrase *"Show up filled up"*. By it he means that when we are prepared for our daily encounters, we should already have something to give away. Far more is accomplished; purpose is honed in on. The necessary awareness to ask the right questions or use the right equipment has already been raised before the event.

It is certainly an essential growth in stature to have made the leap from thinking *"what can I get out of this?"* to *"what can I add to this?"* Pastors and community project leaders know only too well that they rely heavily upon their people's God guidance, self-directedness or

investment as much if not more than their own leadership or inspirational qualities. Especially where there are no financial incentives or little power leverage at the leaders' disposal.

His or her capacity to build team through the emotional investment of the volunteer is paramount for consistent momentum within the organisation. There should be no superstars in church life, though sadly there often are within many religious and charitable endeavours.

However, I shall just get the door. Our penultimate visiting genius, a natural genius at connecting has been ringing for my attention!

COLOSSUS CONNECTOR

Plainly dressed and in keeping with his turn of the eighteenth century outdoor civil engineering project work, Thomas Telford is hesitant about making a grand entrance. He steps quickly inside the threshold and looks around quizzically at the pitched ceiling punctured geometrically with large skylights and festooned with whirly and colourful mobiles. Even for the pioneer of Britain's road and waterway transport infrastructure, the studio is a curious design to behold.

Telford was the son of a shepherd and, like Faraday, he was born into poverty and assigned to a vocational apprenticeship with a stonemason at fourteen years of age. By sixteen he was working in a dockyard and these two formative industries were to direct the course of the rest of his life. Nicknamed *"The Colossus of Roads"*[8], as well as a builder of canals, harbours and bridges all over the British Isles, Telford's legacy was profound.

Although his pioneering work in the use of cast iron in the large-scale construction of bridges and aqueducts was remarkable, I invited him here today to give you the opportunity to grasp how important was Telford's passion for interconnection.

This was the case whether it was to connect one set of remote islanders to another, on the Isle of Arran, or a massive undertaking of the London to Holyhead road project. What seemed to drive Telford was the need to bring communities together and to enhance the ease with which they could travel long distances. He sought to reduce circuitous routes and to pioneer the stable and weatherproof macadam roads that had stronger, smoother, resilient surfaces and made queasy travellers far more comfortable!

Whether by road or waterway, Telford left this island a much more integrated place which was critical to the rise of the nation's wealth and influence in Victorian times. Whether Telford had to build roads from scratch as in the remoter parts of Wales, simply make improvements to existing ones or build brand new harbours as he occasionally did, he was a man of his time that worked at his project until death or until its completion. He had both a vision for interconnectivity as well as generational legacy.

Studio space: *Who do you need to connect together or connect with?*

He asks you now, gently and genuinely *"What are you doing for those that follow?"*

Are you brave enough to undertake some grand scheme that will require years of follow through?

It has been said that the best time to plant a tree is fifty years ago! *"Or even a civil engineering construction,"* Telford corrects me, with a glint in his eye.

Too late? Maybe! But the second best time is now!

What do *you* need to do right now that will bring people together more easily?

With whom can you promote and encourage interdependence and community rather than isolation?

Isolation is one of the most insidious diseases of our generation and whilst we have the most advanced travel and digital communication, it still requires that we intentionally reach out as humans to learn and work together toward a common purpose. For in that endeavour we find that which we need and can give that which others need.

Now who here has a couple of hours?

Who has the patience of a saint and a sharp sense of humour to accompany Telford to the Olympic Park?

Will you take him up the weird and asymmetrical Arcelor Mittal Orbit (aka The Helter Skelter) by Anish Kapoor before we meet our final genius?

7. KNOT OF MADNESS

"I've done it all before!

Been there, done that, got the T-shirt!"

RHYTHM BRINGS RELIEF

You have probably heard that Einstein was attributed with observing that we cannot solve our problems with the same level of thinking that caused them. Or that the definition of madness is doing the same thing over and over again and expecting a different result!

One of my mentors, John Maxwell, puts it like this, *"Sometimes You Win, Sometimes You Learn!"*[1] Genius only emerges as we repeatedly "fail", learn and change accordingly. What maddening cycle must you stop and what new rhythm must you try?

What is this connection between repetition and frustration? Is frustration a cause or an effect of repetition?

With these questions in mind, I can't help thinking about the unfairly stereotypical image of a mentally disturbed individual, rocking, drooling and crouching in a chair or a corner of the room. The nature of madness has been debated for centuries as an illness, a myth or a curse. It still remains something taboo and threatening for the general population.

Yet there is a little of it in us all. Probably a lot - under certain circumstances! Who hasn't found themselves twisting and fiddling with a soaked tissue in moments of sorrow, or pulling at the skin around their nail bed? Or at times realised they had been lost in thought, repeatedly and absentmindedly jerking a thigh or a foot? There is something comforting about cycles of repetition that give us a predictable, if only a minute, degree of control.

A SANE REACTION TO A MAD WORLD?

I was a student nurse in the mid-1980s. In our third year of lectures we were learning about the classical theories of psychiatry and different perspectives on the resilience of the mind. Some claimed that madness is the only sane reaction to the madness of the modern world[2]. We laughed at the longstanding and ironic joke that it was impossible to tell the psychiatric hospital staff from the patients. We wondered anxiously whether we would come out of this placement the same as we entered!

I did not.

Those were the last days of the old institutional mental hospitals before the Community Care Act and the mass closure of psychiatric hospital beds in the UK. My placement at the now demolished remote red brick Victorian Beverley Common hospital *Broadgates* was unsettling. It didn't help that we were heading into the depths of winter, a long term on our most intensive clinical placement of four days a week. The only form of transport for the unearthly seven a.m. start, eight miles from Hull City was on a bicycle along dark unlit lanes, and occasionally through the snow!

That season I was jolted quite unexpectedly into the realisation of the fragility of the human psyche.

Here on a "medium-stay" secure ward for females I came across a woman who in the Second World War had experienced repeated air raid sirens. This had triggered some kind of psychological meltdown and she had been institutionalised ever since, for the last forty years of her life.

Another distressed woman I'll call Teresa spent the day pacing the ward, screaming, wringing her hands, repeatedly trying to undress herself and defaecate on the lino floor. The weekly highlight was her husband's visit with her favourite bag of dolly mixture sweets. She was experiencing some kind of regressive disorder. It was tragic to see her strained husband's helplessness at his wife's torment.

I found it overwhelming as a twenty-one-year-old girl to comprehend the nature of such human distress. Ever since that winter, at such a formative time, the realisation of my own vulnerability has been a source of great strength to me.

When we are threatened, we seek familiarity. This is a basic human reaction in the face of actual danger or distress. We student nurses placed great importance upon our hot dinners and hospital puddings to break up those interminable twelve hour dayshifts! At a few times in my life I have needed and appreciated these very simple and ordinary elements of self-care. This was one of the first of those seasons when a hot meal, a deep sleep, a friend's listening ear and the prayers of a church family were all critical touchstones. It took effort to stay on track in the face of the unfamiliar.

I'm talking about avoiding a full blown fear reaction such as the one I used to experience as a child in my scribbly line nightmare! At some point our resistance can break down though. We know these as emergencies. Invariably everyone around us comes up trumps and makes themselves extremely helpful. We are reminded that in a crisis, it is normal to need the help of others. However, there are times when the necessary helpers don't show up.

My mission to Disentangle Genius is a passion to walk closely on your behalf when you may not have fully grasped the potential and vulnerability you carry. In seeking to undo knots it is always better to work up close, working into rather than pulling away from the tangle, so relieving the tension and loosening the mess.

KNOT of MADNESS - sounds like *"I know! Been there, done that, got the T-shirt"*

This seventh and final knot is a very subtle one. You could almost miss it. Or you could pass it off as insignificant. It looks the same breadth as the strand of thread itself. You could think you might get away without untangling it. Until the strand is caught in a loom or the eye of a needle and will not pass through!

Cycling around and around like a spindle in a repetitious lullaby, you realise after some minutes, months or even years, that you have made no progress. There are no ravelled bands of wool thickening on the bobbin. All this time the very first loop has simply slipped around and around the column without any traction!

RHYTHM BRINGS RELIEF

The essence of madness is to keep doing the same thing and expect a different result!

So, then you must seek to find alternatives, variety and novelty.

Seek to find nuance and degrees of variation.

You may even find yourself seeking distraction and entertainment when your soul is numbed by repetition.

This is a warning.

You need more; you need relief from the false security of routine.

You are falling asleep at the wheel of your lives, sedated, hypnotised by the hum and the spin.

You need the rhythm to escalate rather than merely repeat on the same plane.

You are designed to aspire in ever ascending spirals. Otherwise you continue, deluded or entranced by a plan that has no prospect, exercised by empty endeavour and wondering why you feel a sevenfold frustration.

Genius emerges only as you fail, learn and change accordingly!

What maddening cycle must you stop? What new rhythm will you try?

Because when you are maddened by repetition, you desire
NOVELTY

...... Express Rhythm in a continual flow of fruition............

Only then can you attractively represent the Master through your Genius................

I knew that for our discussion about this knot, the guest genius I had in mind had to be a master at cyclical and escalating rhythm. He was the byword for perseverance and analytical correction by process of elimination. I contacted Thomas Edison, the inventor of the incandescent light bulb!

However, he had heard that the halogen and energy saving light bulbs had taken the corner on the market he once opened up so bravely! After his reputed ten thousand failed attempts to give the world its first electric light bulb he then scaled up manufacture and

made it economically viable for every household to enjoy. Edison graciously acknowledges that technology has now moved beyond even this feat!

Edison wanted to give way for our seventh knot of genius to be modelled by a modern inventor who is still at the forefront of his game. So please welcome your contemporary inventor and entrepreneur, Mr. James Dyson!!

Tall, youthful in visage and with a shock of white hair, James casually eases himself into a revolving and reclining office chair. There is something very compelling and slightly intimidating about his incisive gaze that does not quite sit with his opening statement.

"My life is a life of failure," he jests.

Then I realise he is not joking, he knows that his journey with failure and setback has been his education. That this in itself IS education and the inferior institution of established Western education I have experienced is a very poor substitute for learning by enquiry and experiment.

It is surely a rare gift for one to be able to endure so much frustration and repetition of apparent failure yet still manage to progress a degree closer and closer to an intangible outcome. Every time there is a setback, there is a corresponding new insight or understanding. Every failure is redeemed and recycled into a new insight. This is so different to one who experiences and yet never learns.

BESIDES YOURSELF!

The Greek Biblical word *"paraphronia"* (one of the words for madness, meaning *contrary to the mind*) is found in 2 Peter 2:16 as referring to the Old Testament prophet Balaam. Balaam was known for his lack of convictions and forthrightness as a dodgy consultant. He liked

to look good, however hollow his presentation! Even his own donkey showed greater wisdom than he in digging in its heels on this particular fateful mission![3]

Balaam was cited in this passage as a fickle person who represents the kind who, despite knowing better, returns to wallow in the mud like a freshly washed ignorant pig. Or like a dog, despite physically rejecting a foreign body, it returns to its own vomit. These are powerful images illustrating how abhorrent it is to act in a way that is contrary to revealed truth. It is madness!

Look a little closer and you will see that when Peter is illustrating the folly of the wayward and deceived in the second chapter of 2 Peter, he is comparing them to Balaam. He states that they have once known truth and become **entangled again** (v20).

This word, meaning *to perplex* is the same one used to refer to the need for soldiers to stay focussed on their military duties rather than civilian or domestic affairs (2 Tim 2:20) and the same in Galatians 5:1 where Paul condemns spiritual entanglement: *"do not be hampered and held ensnared and submit again to a yoke of slavery"*. It is critical having once been disentangled that we do not allow ourselves to become perplexed once again!

In order to discover and unveil a potential solution, like Paul, one has to be prepared to admit there is a problem. One has to be prepared again and again. Then, possibly over again, again! For the hundredth or thousandth time you will embark upon a new presentation of a problem! That's progress! Or maybe you tackle the same perplexing enquiry and dialogue. However it really should not be the same conversation with the same people!

Paul, also in 2 Corinthians 11:23, the writer of letters to a different population of new believers states that he is *"Like one distraught"*, (meaning mad) because he is so incensed by their repeatedly falling prey to the false and detracting teachings of other prophets.

This commitment to improvement requires humility.

It is an attribute that James Dyson possesses in spades. Hitting *"Repeat"* is not madness if there is a single spark of novelty to the next level of enquiry, a new variable, a new angle, a new speed or component part!

James says *"I start with what others ignore and make it better"*, going on to explain that his interest in everyday objects has been a secret to his success.

> *"I ask "What do I want?", "What can I leave out?" I use these products myself, I am a user! I always want to make everything neater, smaller, more elegant, even though it's functional. It has to be purposeful AND elegant! This is my trademark and after something in the region of 5,000 prototypes do you not think I will fiercely protect that?"*

In this observant way, every time James brushes his teeth, flushes a toilet or picks up one of his bagless cyclone suction machines, he thinks *"What else?", "What next?"* or *"How?"* He is beautifully curious about and convicted by what others never even notice!

I sense his passion to pass this on to children, young people and invest a heritage of inquisitiveness. Rather he is protecting and defending that quality which children are naturally born with. There's always room for one more question, one more *"What if?"*

Then my jaw gapes open when I hear these words fall out of his mouth.

"It all starts with Frustration!"

I captured it on YouTube[4], check it out for yourself!

I know now, that I have come full circle.

Yet I am starting out again at a higher plane.

Frustration was my enemy.

Now Frustration is my friend!

I can recreate with revived enthusiasm and hope. I have the next iteration in mind and it will be better than the last!

Studio space:

*What significant and incremental change
do you need to make now?*

What can you do differently?

Do you have any idea what you are working *towards*?

What is the next degree of its evolution?

And the next?

And the next?

How will you know when you get to it?

What will help you stay honest?

What will tempt you to settle for "Good enough"?

How will you honour rather than resent frustration in your life from now on?

Can you be friends with frustration?

PART 3:
THE UNTANGLED LIFE

"We are His workmanship"[1]

GENERATE FROM YOUR GENIUS

In Part Three you are going to deepen your exploration into the visual metaphor of untangling. Your truly liberated Genius will be expressed and recreated!

What has been really exciting as I have developed my ideas for this book is the creation itself has been a disentangling and restorative process. Ideas and images, concepts and perspectives from past phases of my life have been garnered. I combined journal extracts, writings, blogs and teachings and earlier reflections from research into the meaning of nursing. All were raw material for this finished statement! It is as if I have disentangled the threads that now blend meaningfully into a tapestry, adding richness and variety, interpretation and ultimately convergence of everything that has come before into one meaningful whole!

For you too I expect the same!

THIS IS THE EXPRESSION OF UNIQUE GENIUS

As you have traced, untangled and aligned your tortuously knotted threads, I am sure that you found much of what you had previously attempted was done with the right intentions. However, a lack of understanding or example, low confidence or the wrong context distorted your vision from becoming reality in the making.

You saw in Part 2, that the untangling of SEVEN coloured knots represents your Tangled Genius on the journey from frustration to freedom.

In attempting to unravel each of these knots, you caused either a tighter, more dysfunctional knotty state or successfully released its untangled counterpart.

These are the respective SEVEN choices or alignments to *liberate your core genius! Seven times we make the choice either to find liberating opportunity or to refrain from it!*

So what are the re-creative possibilities when you tie, knit, crochet, knot, spin or weave these newly aligned threads intentionally? *Let's re-cap the options. You either choose for or against freedom; either against or for frustration!*

CHOOSE NOW! CHOOSE TO LOOSEN OR TIGHTEN THE SEVEN KNOTS OF FRUSTRATION

I hope that defining the Seven Knots of Frustration has stirred you to hope again that there really is such a thing as designed potential rhythm and grace upon your unique genius. For every knot there is a counterpart liberation and creative action! You can experience creative and expressive freedom at every knotty teachable moment!!

Then, Nightmare becomes your Nemesis

Dithering becomes Daring and

extreme Responsibility becomes Recreation!

This is what I discovered and defined. The three threads of black, red and green serve now as the recycled raw material for the expression of creative liberty.

The nightmare in black became the overarching dream and a means to the supreme happiness and fulfilment of flourishing in my OPUS[2]. I call my dream **Disentangling Genius** and it is the anchor and backdrop now of everything I do and decide.

As a result of this anchoring in true hope rather than presumption, wishful thinking or sheer determination, my indecision, embarrassment and dithering was eliminated. Courage was raised as a daring characteristic of my life. The bold blood red thread represents the business I am building called **Motive Leadership**. It tells you that as identity and purpose are clarified, purposeful action can be taken wholeheartedly! This is the confidence that clients and co-workers need to see in yours and my own motivation.

Thirdly and essentially, the green thread of recreation represents the outworking of all that is fruitful, proliferative and life-giving as a result of the strong stance given by the black and red positioning. As a Christian I see this as a **Flow of Fruition**[3] a spiritually inspired and infused outflowing of influence and impact. It may be called ministry by some. In truth it may be impossible to tell the difference between ministry and business as it becomes one coherent masterpiece. I quote the philosopher L.P. Jacks who understood this clearly.

> *"A master in the art of living draws no sharp distinction between his work and his play; his labour and his leisure; his mind and his body; his education and his recreation. He hardly knows which is which. He simply pursues his vision of excellence through whatever he is doing, and leaves others to determine whether he is working or playing. To himself, he always appears to be doing both."*[4]

All is work (when it is meaningful and self-selected) and all is play (truly energising and restorative). Here is the secret of true integrity, combinational, synergistic power with no snagging or snarling, no drudgery, no need for entertainment, escapism or idealism!!

So what will you exchange each of your seven knots or snags for? What does each restorative step look like? Each of the seven knots is undone. For one it might simply have been a case of loosely unlooping, for others it was necessary to have the knot under a magnifying glass to work appropriately and effectively at the taut disarray. You have now taken action at every step; corrective action of the right degree and application to every untangled knot.

1. When you are confused, you need **FAMILIARITY/ ORIENTATION**

.........to follow Pattern and Design...............

The Knot of Confusion requires you to DISCOVER

2. When you are helpless, you need an **EXAMPLE**

...to watch a Demonstration; resource your skill.....

THE Knot of Helplessness requires you to FOLLOW

3. When you are displaced, you need a **CONTEXT**

.... to find your Position; take your stand ....

The Knot of Displacement requires you to LEAD

4. When you are unskilled, you need **ENCOURAGEMENT**

.....enabling proficiency; Function without Frustration...

The Knot of Unskilfulness requires you to EXCEL

5.   When you are stunted, you need **ASPIRATION**

...celebration of Strength; growth to distinctive Stature...

The Knot of Stuntedness requires you to GROW

6.   When you are independent or isolated, you need **COMMUNITY**

.....to give and take, interdependently reproducing Image..

The Knot of Independence requires you to REPRODUCE

7.   And when you are maddened by repetition, you seek **NOVELTY**

......expressing Rhythm in a continual flow of fruition...

The Knot of Madness requires you to RECYCLE and RECREATE

The seven Knots of Frustration blocked and frustrated your every creative intention and desire. Having identified and untangled each one you are now in a position to re-integrate your threads in any way you select. There is

- Weaving

- Sewing

- Tapestry

- Macramé

- Knitting

- Crochet

- Lacemaking

- Embroidery

- Darning

- Felt-making

Let's put one of these into action!

Any of these crafts essentially represents a systematic and patterned form of knotting and tangling: by intention and by design!

Now you can attractively represent the Master through your own particular Disentangled Genius.................

1. SEVEN ALIGNMENTS

"Richard of York gave battle in vain"[1]

Born an "English rose", in the county of Lancashire, at eighteen I left my family home for University, moving to Kingston upon Hull, in a county on the far side of the Pennines mountain range. In the 1980s it was called North Humberside, much to the objection of the local traditionalists. Eventually the council relented and the boundary lines and definition of East Yorkshire were-assigned to the county.

The opening citation above is said to originate from a particularly bloody period of English history: the Wakefield War of the Roses[2] and the defeat and death of Richard, Duke of York. Recalling it probably pains me less than my Yorkshire counterparts, since the House of Lancaster was overwhelmingly victorious!

This familiar mnemonic is a popular saying taught to children to help them remember the initial letters of the seven coloured sequence of the rainbow. However, to avoid reference to this dark chapter of their history, Yorkshire locals wittily adapted their mnemonic to refer instead to one of the successful industries of the region, a world-famous chocolatier, "Rowntrees Of York Gave Best In Value"[3]

Who wants to think that they have battled in vain, that the liberty and satisfaction gleaned from their fight from frustration could be revoked or renounced? No one! Now the task is set for you to stay free and do something with this freedom so that, in the passionate words of St Paul to his friends in Galatia, you

> "stand fast then and do not be hampered and held ensnared and submit again to a yoke of slavery" Gal 5:1[4]

WHAT ARE THE POSSIBILITIES NOW THAT YOU ARE FREE?

We met and marvelled in Part 2 at seven stories of geniuses from history and contemporary life. You chatted to and observed some of the genius greats of the centuries that have gone before. I suggested merely a handful of many possible examples.

One or two were less renowned but all their stories serve simply to show you that everyone has something of value to deposit. Some disentangled their genius more easily than others. They all had their own unique resistors and had to extricate themselves from the pall of obscurity and the curse of entanglement. Due to the opposing, ensnaring and perplexing of the opportunities, comforts, mind-sets and philosophies of their time their geniuses might have been lost to us forever.

Many probably were. We don't know their names.

Too many people allow the cavalcade of resistance to sabotage their best efforts along the course of life. Ultimately it threatens to rob them of their specific influence. Some undoubtedly divert the course of history as a result of their initiative and genius. We will never hear of those who did not or will not. Maybe they will never know or even care what they could have brought.

Will you? My passion is to serve those who know they have *something* to bring. They are actively engaged in resistance against its squashing, thwarting or entanglement. Yes *you can* have a hand in overcoming the likelihood of obscurity and loss to your generation. No one around you or ever after you need then be deprived of your particular genius!!

You too have been baffled or perhaps even battled. You even feared that you had battled in vain like Richard of York. You have faced opposing forces of frustration in your life, though perhaps nothing so overt as an overthrowing of title and throne. Perhaps you moved on, perhaps you hung your head in shame? Or you successfully overthrew the common enemies of fear, indifference, self-doubt and inferiority to go do your "thing". Congratulations!! If not, now is your time!

IT'S NOTHING REALLY!

As a Brit, I know we are poked fun at the world over for our understated-ness and self-effacement. It is one of the unique traits to which we are accultured. It is a curious and incomprehensible feature of ours to those nationals who are more naturally comfortable celebrating their qualities and drawing attention to their attributes. My goodness, we can even struggle to amplify our attributes in necessarily competitive interview situations!!

REALLY?

This is one national characteristic I am determined to refute as it robs us, our families and those in our circle of influence.

And yes, if we believe our strengths are attributed as gifts from God, it robs Him of His glory too!

So in recent years there has been a national popular debate about the nature of *Britishness* along with a supposed sense of lost identity, failing conviction and national insecurity. This is perhaps why in the Opening Ceremony of the London Olympics 2012 the world was left gasping at the scale, panorama and intricacy of the filmmaker Danny Boyle's masterpiece *"Ode to England"*. The New York Times columnist Sally Lyall wrote the day after the *"Isles of Wonder"* spectacle

> *"With its hilariously quirky Olympic opening ceremony, a wild jumble of the celebratory and the fanciful; the conventional and the eccentric; and the frankly off-the-wall, Britain presented itself to the world Friday night as something it has often struggled to express even to itself: a nation secure in its own post-empire identity, whatever that actually is"*[5].

Danny Boyle broke new ground. As a nation we Brits usually like to subtly leave things open to interpretation. He really helped us celebrate and showcase who and what we are, sparking international agreement on his interpretation.

> *"It was neither a nostalgic sweep through the past nor a bold vision of a brave new future. Rather, it was a sometimes slightly insane portrait of a country that has changed almost beyond measure since the last time it hosted the Games, in the grim postwar summer of 1948."* [5]

We got a front seat at the wonderful world premiere of the disentangling of our genius within! We took a giant step forward as a nation in revealing our genius! We publicly celebrated the lessons of our reserve and counter-intuitively poked fun at our quirkiness!

Boyle once told an interviewer about the eclectic range of his films,

"There's a theme running through all of them—and I just realised this. They're all about someone facing impossible odds and overcoming them."[6]

Ode to England celebrated the fascinating depths of a national character that has experienced and overcome frustration!

Consider now, that your nationality is merely one thread contributing to your uniqueness and remarkable complexity. Add in your family upbringing, political or religious influences, educational philosophies and systems and you passively and actively become a product of all these various exposures.

PASSIVE OR ACTIVE

They all speak to us subconsciously until we recognise their presence and invite them to stay or leave. Some of them serve us and some most definitely do not! TED talk sensation, social scientist and shame researcher Brene Brown[7] calls them our gremlins. By identifying that you have accommodated various "gremlins", you can make a choice instead to serve them notice.

Instead of simply incorporating, you can become acutely aware of the nature of these influences and selectively choose which resonate with you and which do not! This could roughly be called personal self-awareness, emotional intelligence and the renewing of the mind about your specific combination of beliefs, unchanging personality traits, character refinement and spiritual growth. This is where you start to pull out some of the threads that were never meant to be part of the design.

Are you beginning to see why we have that saying *"It's all part of life's rich tapestry"*? Unfortunately too many of us allow others to weave and embroider themselves into our lives. Instead of consulting first with your own primary pattern, desire and intended function you invite

other random additions. Whether influences be fundamental and material components or decorative flourishes, seeking integrity and alignment of every single element has to be your lifelong endeavour. Your many traits and attributes are very vulnerable to entanglement.

Now you have discovered the causes of sapped courage and adequacy for your task! Now you can really believe afresh in the possibility of creating life as it is intended. It is vital that you future–proof yourself from the same almighty mess recurring in your life.

This is how I see it.

You have two choices left now. (You already made the first of three, to disentangle!)

PLAY; PLAY BOLD OR PLAY SAFE

Imagine these seven untangled threads lined neatly on your studio counter. It is kind of rewarding to see them all uniquely separated. You arrange them with satisfaction in the order of all the colours of the rainbow. But don't forget, a rainbow is only ever meant to be a whisper, a promise and the hint of assurance you need along your journey.

A rainbow is temporary and fleeting. It is not something you can preserve or capture. Why would you try to hold static what you *purposely* extricated in a moment of time? Now it is time to take new risks, to follow your recovered pattern and design whether it be a new attempt at an original intention or a new design emerging from your original misadventure.

You now stand on the threshold of a new recreation of your life. You either glimpse what could be and re-engage those threads in a new expression or you safely tidy away and freeze your potential in an effort to avoid a similarly confusing episode.

OUT OF THE WORKBOX!

My mother, after she had searched for and used a cotton reel from her sewing box, would rewind, tuck and anchor the stray end securely in the sharply nicked edge of the reel. Then she would line the cotton reels neatly away.

Each one was marked clearly with the manufacturer's label "Sylko *Flame orange*" or "*Coal black*". Now and again she would have a clear requirement for a specific red or turquoise cotton. She conducted a little mending here or replacing of a button there with each carefully matched shade of thread.

Will you now use the various hues of potential you have salvaged from frustration simply for the odd bit of mending, saving and preserving or will you fully aspire to engage all this liberty? Now you can begin a further exciting rendition of imaginative re-interpretation!

Your genius has not been liberated to be merely catalogued and stored but for an expansive, expressive and creative reason!

This is what you have discovered. You already have all the raw materials needed for fulfilment and satisfaction!!

Unlike Richard of York, you do not have to give battle in vain!

THESE ARE THE SEVEN PRECIOUS THREADS FOR ALIGNMENT OF DESIRE WITH EXPRESSION

1. When you are confused, you need FAMILIARITY/ORIENTATION

.........to follow Pattern and Design................

The Knot of Confusion requires you to *DISCOVER*

Harry Beck taught you how to reduce multi-layered complexity into one integrated design.

What have you simplified about yourself?

What did you untie, discard or include within your studio?

What does Harry Beck's immersion in and perseverance with design and improvement to his London Underground map design teach you about consistency, simplicity and essentialism?

Are you ever finished improving the design or workmanship of your life?

Whose pattern are you following?

2. When you are helpless, you need an EXAMPLE...to watch a Demonstration; resource your skill…......

THE Knot of Helplessness requires you to *FOLLOW*

Faraday reminded you of the need for mentors, examples of those who have gone before you. He also became an example and advocate for those who would follow.

Be curious and you will find what you need!

Similarly, anyone with a hint of curiosity deserves your time and attention in return.

Simply help others along their way!

What is your fascination or pursuit?

To what can you apply the lessons of your "bookbinding years"?

Who are you meant to be helping?

3. When you are displaced, you need a CONTEXT

……….. to find your Position; take your stand

The Knot of Displacement requires you to *LEAD*

What did the Great Giotto teach you about your need to look again at what you really see?

And the perspective that you are working with?

Is it possible that you could take a different stance, find a safer place or maybe even a more prominent lead?

Could YOU be the one who breaks a strand of tradition or re-interprets all the clues that have been laid so far?

4. When you are unskilled, you need ENCOURAGEMENT

………..enabling proficiency; Function without Frustration…

The Knot of Unskilfulness requires you to *EXCEL*

Stephen Wiltshire showed us that being unskilled in one area does not necessarily exclude us from the ability to excel somewhere!

There's a special grace on all of for us something!

Who do you remember noticing something special that you could do?

What was that and can you reactivate your gift?

Who might you notice and encourage in turn?

Even the gifted need encouragement to turn unconscious competence into conscious excellence!

5. When you are stunted, you need ASPIRATION

....Celebration of Strength; growth to distinctive Stature.

The Knot of Stuntedness requires you to *GROW*

Florence Nightingale aspired to be a nurse. I simply thought I did.

Can you make that distinction and decide what it is you really aspire to?

What stops you from being visible?

What is the source of nutrition for your growth?

When will you be ready to be revealed on your horizon?

How can you prepare for great prominence?

6. When you are independent or isolated, you need COMMUNITY

......to give and take, interdependently reproducing Image..

The Knot of Independence requires you to *REPRODUCE*

Thomas Telford pursued connection on a grand and national scale.

Do you value community?

What degree of solitude do you also need?

When does solitude become selfish or debilitating?

What changes to your landscape will be needed to allow others' influence upon you and your own upon them?

How carefully do you build relationships and how enduring are they?

To what degree might you need to step up your level of interdependence?

Can you think of something unique that would never have been created without those who worked on it with you?

7. And when you are maddened by repetition, you seek NOVELTY

...... Expressing Rhythm in a continual flow of fruition..........

The Knot of Madness requires you to *RECYCLE and RECREATE*

What is maddening about your life? In other words, contrary to the way you want it?

How have you usually viewed failure?

James Dyson has been called the modern day Edison. How many times do you think it is reasonable to "keep trying"?

Originally, and perhaps like me for many years, you gave battle in vain. Now all seven knots are disentangled.

The indistinguishable confusing mess is liberated and may be woven into three strong and distinct cords with very different names now than those you started out with.

When the first century Christian pioneer St. Paul said of his personal sacrifices and suffering as a missionary

> *"I am already about to be sacrificed [my life is about to be poured out as a **drink offering**]; 2 Tim 4:6* [8]

he was apparently relaxed about the prospect of a wasted life spent with the right motives. I struggled with that statement for many years as it seemed to be incompatible with another Biblical value, that of redeeming the time we have been given.

Yet Paul could confidently give back to his God the sovereign perogative, to have even wasted Paul's life, because he knew completely and confidently that God would never really waste a forensic momentary detail of his life.

Nor will He yours!

The black of your Nightmare becomes the accent of your Nemesis (Disentangled Genius)

The red of your Dithering becomes your Daring (Motive)

The green of your Responsibility becomes your Recreation (Life cycle or Flow of Fruition, in transcendence as community)

These three can now be interwoven purposefully into your own unique and many faceted possibilities that are your GENIUS!

Through the untangling of The Seven Knots of Frustration, DISCOVERED and LIBERATED GENIUS becomes a REFLECTION of GLORY

My unique colour, your unique colour is the suffering of His light! (This is my twist on a famous quotation by Goethe[9]).

2. THREE STRANDS

"A three-fold cord is not easily broken"[1]

Each original strand represents A Nightmare, Daring and Recreation. In Part Two, I outlined a journey through seven knots in the process of disentanglement. You are seeking progress from frustration at one extreme to expressive and creative liberty at the other.

Now disentangled, all the properties of the elements of your eased and aligned life are available to you to re-integrate and create. **Seven** different wools of disentangled and then recreated fibre are produced by spinning them into **three** main strands that will become **one** final cord or expression of your life. It will not then be easily broken! Or frustrated!

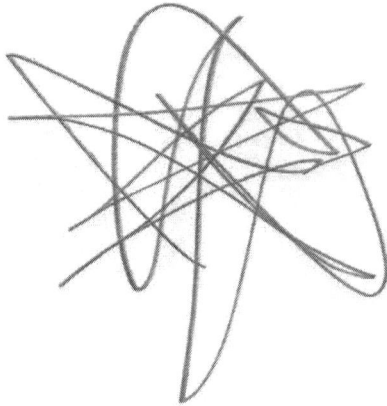

NIGHTMARE BECOMES YOUR NEMESIS

There might have been still another twist in the fibre of my story. In this third and final part of the liberation of your genius, I thought to expand the framework of seven knots of frustration. I would talk about the colours of the artist's palette and detail all seven hues of the visible light spectrum. It was appealing to play with these primary and secondary colours and all the ideas exploding from these concepts.

However, that may be for another book! I too am learning that true Masters simplify, they do not over complicate. I have watched almost passively as some of the concepts of this book evolved. Others were more contrived and did not make it into the pages of the final draft. So I choose to stay true to my spinning metaphor and to those ideas that seem to me to be "inspired" rather than constructed.

BLACK IS BLACK

Remember that within your genius you have three dimensions, the three coloured threads of **Nightmare, Daring and Recreation?**

Why would anyone retain or recycle the freshly disentangled black thread at this new beginning of hope and renewal? Wouldn't you want to get rid of the ugly black thread? Isn't it the imposter in this story of recovery and liberty? In fact it is an accent, a testimony to your incredible escape, in fact it is shame re-interpreted, a strand you need never be ashamed of!

As long as I can remember having the power of imagination, there was that ever present "non-colour" black. It first made its threatening appearance all those years ago as an abstract nightmare, a menacing and angry scribbly line. Later, I was taught that a true artist must never resort to using black for definition. To outline something with a black line is shorthand for saying "I can't represent the real article exactly as it appears so I've outlined the edge of the subject to help you interpret my result".

I used the black outline copiously in my childhood drawings and paintings. I enjoyed the contrast and definition. I loved the neatness and vibrancy it brought to other patches of colour. I was reminded of this two summers ago when I watched an unusual community history project serialised for Channel 4 on British TV.

TAPESTRY REINVENTED

A number of digitally woven tapestries collectively called *The Vanity of Small Differences* was designed and created by Grayson Perry, Turner Prize winning textile artist, Reith lecturer 2013 and insistent transvestite[2]. The documentaries investigated the nature of British "taste". The tapestries Grayson sought inspiration for, were commissioned by the TV channel and arose from his many interviews with everyday people from three distinct social classes; the working class, middle class and upper class.

Of the tapestries, Perry said,

> *The Vanity of Small Differences consists of six tapestries that tell the story of Tim Rakewell. Some of the characters, incidents and objects I have included I encountered whilst filming All in the Best Possible Taste.*
>
> *The tapestries tell a story of class mobility. I think nothing has such a strong influence on our aesthetic taste as the social class we grow up in"*

Why did this unconventional programme grab my attention? I think the way that Perry engaged completely with the different strands of interest it wove was fascinating.

There was the strand of Grayson's philosophising about life and how we represent ourselves. We saw a little of the artist himself, his currency as a contemporary artist, the fact he had used the series to display his flamboyant alter-ego and how he found freedom in this for the first time outside the relatively safe enclave of the accepting and tolerant arts community.

For me this was an awkward, unwelcome and even dark side of a story that represented distastefulness as I see it. Popular media[3] leads us to believe that his feminine identity has caused a rift between himself and his own mother. Yet the use of his exposure and his exploration of our responses to one another's taste was cleverly embodied in his various guises.

Perry also borrowed for each of his tapestries, classical religious themes of the early Renaissance artists such as the annunciation, the adoration of the Magi and the expulsion from the Garden of Eden. These themes point to the underpinning human instincts we still experience, of guilt and shame, the need to worship, to sacrifice and to encounter the miraculous.

There was the storytelling of the rich compilation of community characters from the brash and bold working class of Sunderland and the industrial north and of the carefully understated middle class angst-ridden residents of Kingsmill and Tonbridge Wells. Finally, we peeped into the world of the somewhat faded grandeur of the remnant landed gentry of Somerset.

The most compelling for me was the footage of Grayson elegantly drawing rich and colourful illustrations first in clean black ink, then deftly coloured in with stunning shades. Luscious colours were translated into photo shop digital designs and computer coded Pantone mapping. Six such maps were transformed into incredibly rich, vibrant panoramic tapestries that sang with weighty meaning and recognition, nostalgia and spirituality from the stark, bright white walls of the exhibition. They documented the human condition as ironically as their inspirational source, William Hogarth's series of small paintings *The Rake's progress*[4] depicting the eighteenth century society classes and Tom Rakewell's progressive decline into debauchery.

These tapestries made purposeful use of the power of the black outline reminding me of Cezanne's playfulness with perspective and disregard for depth. In the same way Grayson was playing with the boundaries of our understanding of embedded social norms and expectations whilst at the same time memorialising them in exquisitely observed detail.

These studies, these colours, and these observations were portrayed without reference to the mixture of good and bad; of value and detriment. That is left to the eye of the beholder. We all have a different idea of what good and bad taste looks like.

But can we really afford to define our own life as of a good or bad quality without absolutes and reference points? There has to be an absolute pantone colour reference for any colourist to faithfully reproduce the intended outcome. Any hairdresser, painter and decorator will vouch for that!

Once defined, once disentangled it is so much easier to see what is and what is not adding value to our lives. And even that which

appears dark, ugly or colourless can contradict all established wisdom and contribute the dramatic accent needed in order to accentuate the beauty around it! The difference between ugliness and redemptive style and character is that the dark contrast can now be intertwined purposefully!

BLACK, RED AND GREEN

These three strands are three very distinctive dimensions of existence. They are the threads that once were so knotted and tangled. We are born with inherent beauty and yet brokenness. Without grace we become dysfunctional to some degree or another and may only contribute a fraction of the value we were intended to.

If and when a spiritual crisis reveals and brings recognition to our sheer futility and the impossibility of life without a redeeming God, *then* our opportunities abound! I think artists are the closest to sensing this even without having necessarily come to understand it.

Making purpose out of randomness is something we do understand at a basic level. Ever seen any of the survival programmes or reality shows that cast individuals on a remote island as one of a motley group of strangers fending for themselves through challenge after challenge?

I saw the debut episode of *The Island*[5] recently. The thrust was to run the extreme explorer Bear Grylls' commentary over the exploits of a group of thirteen modern urban men testing their survival mettle on a remote Pacific island.

Having taken around twelve frustrating hours to successfully catch a spark and start a fire, they desperately swigged their boiled, still warm, discoloured and yet safe drinking water. That priority fulfilled, they turned to finding food and it was not long after that before they were gathering reeds and vines to manufacture rude string and ropes.

Fairly early on in any viable community there is a need to be able to tie and bind, hang and connect items with each other! The show was a window on the classic Maslow hierarchy of human needs[6] and an adult twist on William Golding's *Lord of the Flies*[7] in the resultant bid for survival, flourishing and leadership.

Man instinctively needs to create order out of chaos. It is a feature of healthy living to be committed to doing this.

Some people struggle to maintain order and decency even in their physical environment. Now there's another excuse for an addictive reality show, *The Hoarder Next Door!*[8] Why do people keep old bottles and lids, groaning head-height stacks of newspapers, cigarette butts and congealed cartons? Why turn a blind eye to scatterings of dead insects and multiple droppings around the skirting boards or even (heaving slightly) on the kitchen counter? You may feel disgust or sympathy; call it a mental illness or sheer laziness.

Whatever the label, you know something is quite adrift when a home becomes such a hovel. Most of us have had the urge now and again to "have a good clear-out" long before things reach this pitch. Most of us fight the law of entropy vigorously and systematically. It's called dusting and vacuuming, fixing and mending! It's not fun but the results are gratifying.

What if this kind of decay and congestion without regular tending and clearing was going on psychologically within our souls? It's a useful picture for me!

All the great motivational platform speakers and leaders such as Zig Ziglar[9], Steven Covey[10], Tony Robbins[11] and John Maxwell[12] have become renowned for their wisdom in the application of daily small changes for overall momentum to have the slightest chance of occurring. Progress is obscure, it is boring, it receives no attention...until it has been neglected for long enough.

Then a major "house clearance" has to take place with all the attendant risks that many valuable items may be lost in the melee. It is simply too much trouble to sift through! That was supposed to happen daily.

At least when a lost earring rattles up the vacuum nozzle you can usually notice, stop and rescue it immediately. But when the room is literally bursting with trash, the chances of being reconciled with anything mislaid are microscopic!

What treasures of yours may be buried in the dust of unexploited experience? I would say that I had always considered myself organised, careful to steward wisely the things that I owned and the opportunities I encountered. However, a niggling feeling that all was not well grew and grew until I realised that much of what I had accumulated simply had "accumulated" and not been applied.

I was the soul equivalent of *The Hoarder Next Door* and it was time I risked putting the catalogued resources to good use instead of simply preserving them. So I seriously embraced the task of writing for others rather than myself!

Inevitably when we sort our clutter there will be dust, lots of it.

Sometimes I can be overcome with an urge to clear, remove, re-order and de-clutter. Suddenly the prospect of moving a picture from one room to another crosses my mind. At last I see that a battered set of drawers is really not worth keeping, that a bulky filing cabinet can be squeezed off the landing to open up the space completely!

One week I was doing this very thing. I had also been reading the book *Necessary Endings* by Henry Cloud[13] and had had my eyes opened to the fact that I am *really* not good at seeing endings and conclusions (prunings) as a part of normal, seasonal life. It's why I hoard old cards, books, games I have lost pieces of and CDs I never listen to any more! Never afraid of change or innovation (I love it) it was quite a surprise to realise that I also obviously needed to habitually let go of something if I expected to progress along new paths. Which things was I to let go of and which should I hold on to? This is something we all have to learn both in our physical environments and our relationship space.

However, this applies equally to our mental clutter.

My friend, Kary Oberbrunner, believes in something along the lines of *"doing it scared"*, or *"jump and build your wings on the way down"*. We must refuse to be paralysed by possibilities and analysis, refuse to procrastinate until we think we know everything we need to know about something before we can possibly try! That's when we find out what we need to know!

When we start to act upon an idea, a motive or a passion, even when we don't know *How*, God has a habit of putting things in our way that resource and equip us to find out just that! Wisdom comes through experience. It's only when we start to dislodge and re-order that we remember even half of what we know and have and could now do with! I am constantly amazed at how often when I am looking for one mislaid item, I find something else equally useful and timely just because I was alert and actively looking.

Now, instead of resisting and resenting the disruption of periodic clearances, my somewhat fragmented concentration is permitted to flit from one thing to another. It's the equivalent of a tea-break in the middle of gardening!

For instance, during a few weeks of serious writing, I had a sequence of house improvements to my hall and stairway. I watched my decorator Kev smooth out the rich gold wall covering and replace the worn terracotta paper. As I appreciated the simple white gloss brightening up the chipped and yellowed paintwork, he teased me about my past propensity to overdo the colour! He was *"neutralising me"* he joked! Now that will *never happen* but I did like the idea of simplifying and making classy what was a rather tired bohemian look!! The light,

bright new hallway announced to my friends and family that I was cleaning up my act, after a rather too messy and uneasy association with the familiar.

It can be very disruptive having workmen in the house. However, instead of resenting my altered schedule and freedom, I decided to simply "go with the flow".

One day I attended a medical appointment, spent more time in the company of my daughter and drove her to an interview. I gave my son extended attention every evening whilst he rehearsed revision exam answers! I pulled dandelions and rampant weeds, polished a piece of neglected furniture, had a haircut, ordered a spare part for a vacuum cleaner, renewed my car insurance and ordered heavy goods online for delivery. I trusted it as an opportunity for reading and reflection, as fodder for more and more ideas and insights yet to form. And I made good some commitments that needed confirming.

Now, although I am far from expert at disentangling myself from the old and mundane, I absolutely embrace the new and the novel! What I have done is get a little bit better at seizing the moment. I have ruthless clarity about what is and is not necessary for the life I envision. It is very refreshing.

Such pruning and what Henry Cloud calls a *"good hopelessness"*[13] about the redundant and merely sentimental, has been stirred in me. Now I aim to keep alert to this awareness and exercise the courage to allow my overwhelming "Yes" to dictate to and cut off the inevitable "No's" I have been tripping over in my hallway, living space and perhaps my emotional and thinking space for far too long.

EMBARRASSING DITHERING IS TRADED FOR DARING

I remember the art teacher I had, when I was six years old. (She did not deserve to be an art teacher. It was more likely she was a teacher

who happened to take the art lesson). She handed out everyone's piece of work from a previous lesson. These were brittle and powdery with "too much paint" she complained." *And whose is this?"* she glowered threateningly.

It would soon be evident that I was the only one who didn't have a painting. I had to admit it was mine. *"That is such a waste of paint"* she decried.

I was taken aback. I had thought it a very expressive and enjoyable technique. We had discovered all by ourselves the pleasure of jerking our brushes to cause firework-like spatterings of colour all over our oblong sugar papers. I was genuinely shocked and confused that it was deemed unacceptable. It was probably one more little dent in my willingness to risk doing something exploratory. It was a little bit more scaffolding added to the construction of my fear of disapproval. It was another reason why I felt excited to discover the American Jackson Pollock's crazy canvasses many years later![14]

Thankfully, I didn't stop painting but I think I mostly stopped daring.

The last few years of my life have been a retrieval of that original courageous spirit I once lost!

OVERWHELMING RESPONSIBILITY GIVES WAY TO RECREATION

After my childhood ability in creative writing and accomplishing an A level English grade "A" I was in for a great shock early on in my University training. I was rattled when the penny dropped that I was expected to write impartially about "phenomena" from a third party, balanced and critical perspective.

Analysis of literature such as *"Middlemarch"* by George Eliot[15] and Austen's *"Emma*[16] gave the freedom to respond and comment from

a personal perspective. I was somewhat appalled by our first year, first term research critique assignment. We were to present a seminar on a research classic by the name of *"Bowel Function in Hospital Patients"*[17]! The joy of writing, finding, using and incorporating metaphors, personal impressions and responses was almost lost to me after four years of this etiquette and typical subject matter!

Scientific research methodology, dispassionate treatment of one's instincts, logical hypothesis testing or unbiased attempts to disprove a hunch actually flew in the face of my natural desire to describe and engage with and synthesise an experience.

After many years of largely academic reading and writing eventually I wanted to own my personal perspective once again. It took a little longer to lose my self-consciousness (a form of pride); discomfort as a result of disclosure.

Once I accepted I had every right to reclaim my writing, I was free of the traditional responsibility to be balanced, guarded and unbiased. I could own my perspective and then offer it. Take it or leave it, it was mine and in giving it away I was recreating myself! Work became play! Disciplines of style had only been necessary so that I could understand now, how and where and why to bend the rules, how to knot new alignments again in fresh and unique formations!!

The great eighteenth century socialist activist, textile designer, poet and novelist William Morris understood perfectly the need to strip everything down to its essentials. Not merely factual essentials though! He was quite clear that we should leave room for aesthetics in our lives as an absolute requirement. He was famous for saying

> *"Have nothing in your houses that you do not consider to be beautiful or functional."*[18]

Beauty, attractiveness, the unquantifiable and emotive has reason to be found in every corner in our lives. I celebrate its prominence in all

of its anecdotal, biased unbalanced and unique glories! I don't think we really come close to appreciating this until we have at least once been hopelessly tangled up in life's tiresome knots of uniformity, bureaucracy and utility.

Then, like Fallen Adam (as an unblemished and infallible angelic being can never hope to understand) we will gratefully appreciate everything that is restored to us afresh!

True beauty is to have purposeful, rhythmical and aspirational function.

True beauty is to reflect glory and attract and engage others in that way of being.

All three strands are ready to be combined effectively into one unique declaration.

3. ONE CORE

"Where is the child in me - don't die!
Come alongside all else I am
Catch up with me again"[1]

Beautiful attraction

We, the Disentangled should be the most beautiful, colourful people on earth! We know that on at least seven levels, Frustration knotted our beauty; strangled and contained it inaccessibly until something, someone, somehow had the opportunity, knowledge, the skill and desire to help us to release us.

BEAUTY ENTANGLED

Allow me to put my conversation so far, right into a context I believe it belongs to.

There was once a tree in the middle of the Garden of Eden[2], the first home of mankind. God told Adam that he was not to eat the fruit of this Tree of the knowledge of good and evil. As Christians believe and as many have heard about, Adam took this fruit from Eve and knowingly disobeyed God's instruction. By eating it, in a moment there was a legal right activated.

Adversarial knots of frustration crept in and tied him up. This snare tightened around his very life, health, relationships, potential and productivity. He died spiritually, his life source and intimate connection with God was cut off and a genetic bondage called sin entangled him and his descendants, forever.

Another tree in Eden, the beautiful and attractive Tree-of-Life had once been a place of accessible refreshment, healing and integrity. Now its fruit were a dangerous threat to the sin and death-bound mortals Adam and Eve.

God provided an Angel to guard it and to protect its fruit from being picked prematurely. He needed to protect Adam and Eve from being immortalised within this new struggling fallen and frustrated state[3]. As their descendants, we needed to be stayed from becoming eternally and irreparably separated from God. Only after renouncing the foolishness of originally disobeying God could it become possible again to access this freedom. Only as repentant mortals could we be safely permitted to resume eating the Tree of Life.

This is a grand and beautiful example of Frustration being our path to Salvation. God is the Master at keeping us from something until the very moment we can benefit from it. You cannot break a law, said Stephen Covey, you can only break yourself against it[4]! We need to be held firmly, lovingly and prohibitively from self-destruction through premature fulfilment of desire.

When I was learning about the story of James Dyson I knew he *had* to be the one I invited to your studio as a modern manifestation of the seventh redeemed knot of madness. He certainly understood a truth which many of us fail to see, least of all embrace.

"Frustration is your Friend!"

Talk about a teachable moment! That was a biggie for me. *"That's it!"* I exclaimed excitedly, *"Thank you James, Thank you!"* I squealed when I heard him say this on a You tube videoclip[5] about failure.

WAKING THE PRINCESS

Once I despised frustration as a regular imposter in my life. Frustration was not my friend, it was a fiend! Once, you and I were caught in a conspiracy to thwart our flourishing. You and I were a sleeping Princess. A Princess condemned to sleep in a nightmare of frustration. Now you are not a sleeping Princess. You are awake and beautiful to behold. However this was no sudden or passive awakening at the kiss of your long awaited suitor.

You purposefully and deliberately offered yourself to an apparently laborious but trustworthy process of disentanglement.

Somewhere along the line, very late I would say, I realised life is not sectioned neatly into two periods of preparation and readiness. It was a slowly dawning shock to me, to find that I have never seemingly passed an obvious threshold or felt there was a moment I was ready for adulthood! In fact there probably never will be!

Are you still waiting to be "enough"? You will find that you continue to experience evolving transient, developmental cycles.

Then there is a moment you understand you only have NOW and that THEN depends on NOW. Then you realise that NOW does not depend on THEN and at last you can start to relax. When you realise there are often second and third chances and that reiteration brings new depths of understanding, you are in less of a hurry to achieve and rather, simply appreciate.

ATTENTION TO BEAUTY

I have a friend who lives in a high degree of appreciation of every moment. Her children have a family joke about her tendency to break off momentarily announcing *"Oh, Look at that dog!"*, or *"Isn't that beautiful?"* Though they pull her leg each one of them realises they are indebted to her for inheriting a deep appreciation of nature and beauty.

This is a testament to her commitment to live above the daily grind of familiar frustrations. She learned this whilst fulfilling a selfless role as a Mom. Home-schooling, carpooling, cake baking and home-making, she was never quite sure she hadn't denied something of her own calling. To what, she didn't know except that she grew to recognise the depth of value and the legacy she had invested in her children.

A quarter century later, I wrote in a Cape Cod seaman's cottage with muted blue décor, crusty painted doors and white plaster panelling. I worked on the final chapter of my first book whilst enjoying a lengthy and perfectly conceived holiday with her family in MA, New England. My wonderful hosts and friends of old are a beautiful couple in their late fifties. Originating from Sri Lanka they entered my life in the late eighties when as a single woman I enjoyed entertaining her young children. My friend and I had fellowship after their bedtime whilst her anaesthetist intern husband was absent for long hours on call at Hull Royal Infirmary.

Like me, and like any couple, they have had their own cycles of frustration and fulfilment. To be the sole recipient of their generous hospitality for the first time since my own entanglement and liberation is incredibly humbling, heart-warming and refreshing. It is poignant, to be here and single once again in the same generous company after divorce and recovery from many frustrated dreams.

Their daughter remembers that I was her childhood grown-up friend who gave her many memorable "first time" experiences. There was

the first cinema visit to *"Honey I shrunk the Kids"*[6], the first sleepover and her first (and probably last) taste of rabbit stew!! Now as an animated and highly cultivated professional young woman, she is assisting her mother and father in giving me a round of first experiences in return.

I have seen my first wild seals in the Atlantic Ocean and drunk my first ever Margarita! I have tasted Reese's peanut butter cups and Falafel "chips", have been to a painting party and attended a roaring twenties costume Lawn dance. Here at The Crane Estate's ocean view setting amongst an enthusiastic crowd of vintage clothed picnickers I felt more English than I have ever felt at home!

All of this is a beautiful experience of the enriching cycle of life or the proverb *"What goes around, comes around"*. Nothing ever goes to waste and each of us are living proof of the fact that if we will dare to live generously we will receive abundantly. Conversely, if we hold onto disappointment, withhold, restrict and begrudge others their chance, the same scarcity is dealt back to us. I firmly believe this.

Like attracts like! We disentangle, align, integrate and then magnify one another.

In a life of community we are collectively restored to the image of God. It is as it was always intended, as if it had never been otherwise. And yet, because of the "otherwise" we are all the more useful. Where uniqueness intersects with uniqueness, genius shines forth in inconceivable ways!

We are clothed with original beauty, becoming new – vintage creations

BEAUTY COVERED

We were filled with the knowledge of good and evil and discriminated along such lines. We created a set of codes and behaviours

to define what was acceptable and what was not. True hope became lost. So God made animal skin clothing to preserve man's dignity[7]

Adam was now spiritually dead, there had to be a reversal of his condition before God could allow him access to eternity. Religion was born and the law in all its weakness was written to expose the inadequacy of externally ruled hearts. It was an act of overlooking grace, dignifying the human race and heralding the future sacrifice of His Son Jesus. For generations to come through the prophets and priests God made it clear that mankind could not access his Presence[8] could not be forgiven without sacrifice. God was obliged to do this, both to protect His own holiness and ourselves from living eternally in a fallen state or from being extinguished by His purity.

In the first instance, laws and boundary lines were given to protect mankind from self-destruction or anarchy. I might call it Total Frustration. That is why God introduced rules and restrictions, always anticipating that it would dawn upon us that we could never pass the test unaided. We could never be good enough and only God could change us; we could not change ourselves.

Amongst inferior Religion and all the variations of a "religious" theme, hope would spring from frustration. Hope against all hope is your rediscovery that relationship and not religion is the intended design and your only access to liberty.

TOUCHING THE VOID

The power of attraction has been thoroughly explored by popular psychology[8] today. As a principle it is powerfully effective. I interpret religious tradition as an obstacle that often frustrates your attraction of others. It is a striving, anxiety-ridden repulsion that obscures the beauty of the life of Christ within. Frustration, as one expression of brokenness is a condition that you may arrive at gradually and slowly or suddenly and intensely. It is a spiritual rite of passage that is very attractive to God.

I would like to call it *Touching the Void*. This is reference to an incredible account of mountaintop survival that unfolded in 1985. Two mountaineers tackled the unclimbed West face of the fearsome 21,000ft Siula Grande in the Peruvian Andes. Having slipped on a ledge, Joe Simpson's companion Simon faced the terrible decision to cut the rope by which he too was being pulled by Joe's weight, into certain oblivion[10].

Agonisingly choosing the lesser of two evils he purposefully cut the lifeline by which Joe precariously hung. His trusted companion plummeted into the yawning belly of the mountain. Beyond help, beyond sight, sound and even hope. Simon disentangled himself from Joe and certain death, to prevent two inevitable deaths rather than one. Joe fell impossibly deeply into the crevasse. Waking bewilderedly, miraculously, some unmeasured time later Joe found himself caught upon an internal ledge. Somehow an inevitably fatal fall was interrupted! Yet now, Joe was even more horribly inaccessible to would-be rescuers. After agonising for hours over the irony of not having being killed yet lost beyond help, Joe silently rolled off the ledge toward certain death. He had the choice of sudden or slow death; a choice between oblivion or fatal solitary confinement.

When we dare to recognise the yawning and awful emptiness of our own efforts, we cut our losses and fall impossibly, touching the void of our total emptiness and inability.

This is where we are miraculously caught and gratitude and intimate desire for life wells up again. But we are not to remain paralysed in the void once we have touched it. In fact after Joe's deeper and suicidal second fall, he miraculously found himself in an escape shaft that led him out to into the sunshine of a lower slope of the Siula Grande!

Watchman Nee[11] the great Chinese theologian who suffered twenty years in solitude and confinement for his faith, wrote that the spirit of trust is essential to prayer. Suddenly prayer becomes one's vital breath and hope rather than an obligatory guilt ridden exercise. It is now located in the intimacy and availability and power of God to lift us from who, what and where we are. Locating the way of escape, disentangling the genius within AND re-creating it with absolute boldness is now an absolute urgency for ourselves and those who need to hear about this encounter.

What will it take to teach us who we are in God?

His Word and His Voice through the church speaks into our lives. But we wait for the third voice of circumstance! As unbelieving believers we believe in God yet not believe His Word! If we dared to go with that call to trust and obey and quelled the fear deep within, we would be brought face to face with our own inadequacies.

We would admit that our life is in the clutch of inevitable death. There we are trapped and caught within a grave beyond rescue. Too damaged to climb out, we are also too weak to hold on. We are frightened we might descend deeper into a habit, a lifestyle, a relationship or ill health. Not knowing how to climb out of that hole we are terrified of being separated from the reality we dream of. We remember that hope deferred makes our heart sick. Yet if we hope, Hope does not disappoint us!

> This is why it says: "When he ascended on high, he led captives in his train and gave gifts to men." (What does "he ascended" mean except that he also descended to the lower, earthly regions? He who descended is the very one who ascended higher than all the heavens, in order to fill the whole universe.)[12]

True genius is the promise for all of those who are disentangled to the end of themselves and find a richer, precious experience of liberty as a result.

Now there is a rest and fulfilment in Him that is nothing to do with the circumstances. You can submit to the fact of your incapability and descend into your own inadequacy to discover that the real way of escape is often farther below and deeper and more inaccessible than anything you could ever lose or fear.

Jesus descended so that we could ascend and *there is no place lower than where he has already been.* If there was, everybody there would be beyond his reach. But there is no character too depraved, no sinner too sinful, no sabotaging act too powerful to snarl up anyone's access to God if they want it. And the great news for visionaries held in some knot of doubt and fear, is that there is no call so impossible that God would not equip you for, that He would ask of you without providing a way of expression for you. But the way is not above where you came from, it is below!

It is to lean into the knot, to cut your losses and fall.

CORE BEAUTY

What are you going to do now with your one re-integrated cord?

Maybe it is a lifeline, a piece of rigging or the drawstring of a sumptuously beautiful evening bag. What once had no strength or power, shape or capacity can now position or carry items of great value or purpose!

> Now you have discovered your design, found examples to follow.

> Now you have found the position from which to lead

Now you are encouraged by your excellence

Now you can see how to grow in height and stature

You have seen how integrated others are to you and you are to them

You recognise your need for new degrees of alignment every single day in this courageous life cycle of recreation.

So I ask you something in the last faith-filled words of the mighty Israelite King David who was no stranger to frustration.

Even on his deathbed, he had come to terms with the fact that his lifelong aspiration to build a new Temple was something he now had to delegate to his son Solomon,

"Is not (your) house right with God? Has he not made with (you) an everlasting covenant, arranged and secured in every part? Will he not bring to fruition (your) salvation and grant (you your) every desire?[13]

Touch that void and nothing can ever tangle you again!

FINAL WORD

"A humble exhibition"

I was about eleven, one wet summer holiday evening in the Lake District when I saw an alarming evening documentary about deforestation and climate change. It shook my security in the world as I knew it and as I had always expected it to be.

Another day, it dawned upon me that I loved people even though I didn't really like nursing. It took a lot longer and many setbacks too to realise that I loved the growth of the Kingdom of God even though it was killing me to be leading a particular local church vision.

I also gained total assurance that God loved me personally and far more than my tough commitment to stay married in a toxic relationship.

And later, I remembered that I loved writing even though all of my published writing had been of a stuffy institutionally dictated format.

Things can and do change, whether we ignore this fact or try to make them change ourselves. Some things are within our power to change and some are not. We simply must make the distinction and work with what is and pray about what is not. In this we find our genius and confidently make a humble exhibition of ourselves!

Disentangling will never be completely finished for us; it was only finished in Him!

Our frustration now need only be temporary, a friend to remind us of all current and ultimate possibility.

> *[the Spirit which] you have now received [is] not a spirit of slavery to put you once more in bondage to fear, but you have received the Spirit of adoption [the Spirit producing sonship] in [the bliss of] which we cry, Abba (Father)! Father!*

> *The Spirit Himself [thus] testifies together with our own spirit, [assuring us] that we are children of God.*

> *And if we are [His] children, then we are [His] heirs also: heirs of God and fellow heirs with Christ [sharing His inheritance with Him]; only we must share His suffering if we are to share His glory.*

> *[But what of that?] For I consider that the sufferings of this present time (this present life) are not worth being compared with the glory that is about to be revealed to us and in us and for us and conferred on us!*

> *For [even the whole] creation (all nature) waits expectantly and longs earnestly for God's sons to be made known [waits for the revealing, the disclosing of their sonship].*

> *For the creation (nature) was subjected to frailty (to futility, condemned to frustration), not because of some*

intentional fault on its part, but by the will of Him Who so subjected it—[yet] with the hope

That nature (creation) itself will be set free from its bondage to decay and corruption [and gain an entrance] into the glorious freedom of God's children[1]

May your studio become a familiar place of expression, expectancy, alignment fulfilment, and hope again!

"That's the good part, you get to go find a new dream"[2]

ACKNOWLEDGEMENTS

I am deeply grateful to the people who have made this publication possible.

Thank you, Julie Muleba for your proofreading skills. And to Caroline Taylor and Ruth Gough for welcoming me into their world of wool!

I thank my parents Bentley and Freda. They have always demonstrated true compassion for people and commitment to their community. I am thankful for their persevering spirits and their belief in me when doubts were cast.

To Brian and the late Lilian Taylor I am so grateful for their pastoral care and spiritual investment during my student days and early adulthood.

To Kary Oberbrunner, Brian Butcher, Pete Causton, Mike Coote, Dave Evans, Matthew and Donniece Greene-Smith and Michael Croft I so appreciate you betting on me when business development was a bewildering new landscape.

I especially thank my courageous two children Esme and Simeon who have accepted my regular closeting in the office for many hours at a time. They have grown in independence, trusted me in adversity and believed in me - that all my long term endeavours would eventually align!

I love you and I am proud of your patience!

ABOUT THE AUTHOR

Gill Scott is an author, coach, facilitator and speaker. She helps survivors of frustration, disappointment and loss to disentangle their genius into freedom so that they can release their vital and timely purpose.

Prone to difficulty making major decisions she has gradually developed a keen sense of discernment for underlying patterns, principles, and motives, always seeking to make sense of everything within its context and purpose.

Frustration was once the byword for her life and having analysed it so thoroughly she is able to recognise the knotty patterns and tangled interpretations that cloud judgement, obscure potential and strangle one's *joie de vivre*.

Having salvaged her love of writing and creative communication Gill is creating a new niche as an author and leadership facilitator. She lives in northern England with a courageous teenage son and beautiful adult daughter. Gill serves a growing tribe of The Disentangled (of which you must be one!)

She looks forward to refining this purpose and to help others transcend to tell and live their stories, having identified with hers!

Connect with Gill at: DisentanglingGenius.com

Disentangling Genius

Coaching services

Undo The Seven Knots of Frustration™

to help you unravel your story

And start to align *your* desire with its expression!

Disentangling Genius is a Coaching Programme for the Tangled

Eight weeks of group coaching will equip your "craft studio space" with the tools and resources you need to create your masterpiece, the rest of your untangled life!

- α **Online**
- α **Virtual group**
- α **Face to face**
- α **Exclusive, executive 1:1**

We have a programme to suit your needs and budget

Visit **disentanglinggenius.com**

Disentangling Genius

Corporate or Community

Bring Gill's genius to your team!

to help you make sense of your intent

Facilitator.

Coach. Speaker.

HOST OF CREATIVE RETREATS

Contact Gill today to bring her into your organisation

DisentanglingGenius.com

DisentanglingGenius

Products and Resources

Author's second book *"As If"*

Bespoke Retreat experiences

Expanded Studio Sketchbook

Complementary Programme Journal

Seven Knots of Frustration ™ product range

Thwarted Prodigy™ kits

Gifts for all ages and a range of niches

Available through DisentanglingGenius.com

STUDIO
SKETCHBOOK

STUDIO SKETCHBOOK

STUDIO SKETCHBOOK

STUDIO SKETCHBOOK

STUDIO SKETCHBOOK

STUDIO SKETCHBOOK

STUDIO SKETCHBOOK

STUDIO SKETCHBOOK

STUDIO SKETCHBOOK

NOTES

Introduction

Part 1 Tangled

[1] Virginia M. Axline, *Dibs in Search of self* (Harmondsworth: Penguin, 1964) 20.

Chapter 1

[1] Steven Spielberg, *The War Horse*, movie. (Dreamworks studios: Universal City CA, 2011)

Chapter 2

[1] dare, http://www.merriam-webster.com/dictionary/dare?show=0&t=1409565024, accessed Sep 1, 2014

2 Psalm 105:18, https://www.biblegateway.com/passage/?dc=3&utm_expid=13466113-10.DRY5Q0U2TpaXvRe49bTgCA.3&search=Psalm+105%3A18&version=AMP&utm_referrer=https%3A%2F%2Fwww.biblegateway.com%2Fquicksearch%2F%3Fquicksearch%3DEden%26qs_version%3DAMP, accessed Aug 28, 2014

3 Proverbs 13:12, https://www.biblegateway.com/passage/?dc=3&utm_expid=13466113-10.DRY5Q0U2TpaXvRe49bTgCA.3&search=Prov+13%3A12&version=AMP&utm_referrer=https%3A%2F%2Fwww.biblegateway.com%2Fpassage%2F%3Fdc%3D3%26search%3DPsalm%2B105%253A18%26version%3DAMP, accessed Aug 28, 2104

4 Kary Oberbrunner *Your Secret Name* (Zondervan: Grand Rapids Michigan, 2010)

5 Gen 28:16, https://www.biblegateway.com/passage/?dc=3&utm_expid=13466113-10.DRY5Q0U2TpaXvRe49bTgCA.3&search=Gen+28%3A16&version=AMP&utm_referrer=https%3A%2F%2Fwww.biblegateway.com%2Fpassage%2F%3Fdc%3D3%26search%3DProv%2B13%253A12%26version%3DAMP, accessed Aug 28, 2014

6 John Maxwell Team, http://www.johnmaxwellgroup.com/, accessed Aug 28, 2014

7 Acts 5: 20, https://www.biblegateway.com/passage/?dc=3&utm_expid=13466113-10.DRY5Q0U2TpaXvRe49bTgCA.3&search=Acts+5:17&version=MSG&utm_referrer=https%3A%2F%2Fwww.biblegateway.com%2Fquicksearch%2F%3Fquicksearch%3Dtake%2Byour%2Bstand%26qs_version%3DMSG, accessed Aug 28, 2014

Chapter 3

1 Henry David Thoreau in M. P. Donahue, *Nursing: The Finest Art: An illustrated History* (Mosby: St Louis, 1996)

[2] Nemesis definition, nem·e·sis noun \'ne-mə-səs\: an opponent or enemy that is very difficult to defeat., http://www.merriam-webster.com/dictionary/nemesis?show=0&t=1409243475, accessed Aug 28, 2014

[3] Kim Manley *Exploring Expertise Expertise in Practise (Pilot)* (Royal College Of Nursing: London, 2002)

[4] Morva Fordham and Virginia Dunn. *Alongside the patient in pain. Holistic Care and Nursing Practice* (Balliere Tindall: London, 1994)

Part 2 Knotted

[1] Philippians 2.13 (*bold and italics, author's own*)

[2] Firestarter, (NLP Business course) http://www.realleadershipuk.com/ accessed Sep 5, 2014

Chapter 1

[1] Harry Beck, https://www.tfl.gov.uk/corporate/about-tfl/culture-and-heritage/art-and-design/harry-becks-tube-map, accessed Sep 1, 2014

[2] Joseph Heller, *Catch 22* (Vintage: London, 1994)

[3] Edgar Yipsel Harburg, Somewhere over the Rainbow lyrics from *The Wizard of Oz* movie (Metro Goldwyn Meyer: Beverley Hills CA, 1939)

[4] Henry David Thoreau, *Walden* (Bramhall House: New York, 1951)

[5] Lyman Frank Baum, *The Wonderful Wizard of Oz* (George M. Hill Co: Chicago and New York, 1900)

Chapter 2

[1] Jacob and Wilhelm Grimm, Rumplestiltskin in *The Complete Grimm's Brothers Fairy Tales* (Kindle DX version) retrieved from Amazon.com, 2012

[2] Martin M. Broadwell, Origins of Conscious Competence model (1969) http://www.businessballs.com/consciouscompetencelearningmodel.htm#conscious-competence-theory-origins, accessed Aug 28, 2014

[3] The concept of apprenticeship, http://en.wikipedia.org/wiki/Apprenticeship, accessed July 29, 2014

[4] Michael Faraday, *The Chemical History of a Candle*, (William Crookes, ed. *A Course of Six Lectures on the Chemical History of a Candle*. Griffin, Bohn & Co: London, 1861) http://www.gutenberg.org/ebooks/14474, accessed Sep 1, 2014

Chapter 3

[1] Henry Cloud and John Townsend, *Boundaries* (Zondervan: Grand Rapids Michigan, 1992)

[2] Henry Cloud, *Necessary Endings* (Harper Collins: New York, 2010)

[3] Watchman Nee, http://www.watchmannee.org/life-ministry.html, accessed Aug 28, 2014

[4] Viktor Frankl, *Man's Search for Meaning* (Beacon Press: Boston, 1984) 87

[5] Ezekial 17: 22-24, https://www.biblegateway.com/passage/?search=Ez+17&version=AMP, accessed Aug 28, 2014

[6] Gill Scott, *Flow of Fruition* (Unpublished)

[7] Gill Scott, *She Dares* (Unpublished)

[8] Giorgio Vasari, *The Lives of the Artists*, Giotto (Dover Publications: New York, 2005)

[9] Ernst. H. Gombrich, *The Story of Art* 13th edition (Phaidon: Oxford, 1972)150

[10] Steven Spielberg, Director *Jurassic Park* movie (Amblin Entertainment, Distributed by Universal Pictures CA, 1993) based on Michael Crichton's book *Jurassic Park* (1990)

Chapter 4

[1] Unction, http://www.biblestudytools.com/dictionary/unction/, accessed Sep 1, 2104

[2] K'nex, a creative construction toy by K'NEX Brands, LLC.

[3] Catherine Bailey *Black Diamond* (Penguin: London, 2007)

[4] Kary Oberbrunner, *The Deeper Path* (Baker Books: Grand Rapids Michigan, 2013)

[5] Isaiah 45:3, https://www.biblegateway.com/passage/?search=Is+45%3A3&version=AMP, accessed Sep1, 2014

[6] John C. Maxwell, *The Five Levels of Leadership* (Hachette Book Group: New York 2011)

[7] Jamie Oliver, *Jamie's Kitchen* (Talkback Productions: Channel 4 UK, 2002)

[8] Stephen Wiltshire, http://en.wikipedia.org/wiki/Stephen_Wiltshire, accessed August 28, 2014

Chapter 5

[1] Wingham Wool Works, http://www.winghamwoolwork.co.uk/content/13-about, accessed Aug 28, 2014.

[2] Marianne Williamson, *A Return to Love: Reflections on the Principles of a Course in Miracles* (Harper Collins: London, 1992)

[3] Jeremiah 30:21b, https://www.biblegateway.com/passage/?search=Jeremiah+30.+21&version=TLB, accessed 28 Aug, 2014

[4] Florence Nightingale, *Notes on Nursing: What it is and what it is not* (Kindle DX version) retrieved from Amazon.com, 2010

Chapter 6

[1] Sleeping Beauty, http://en.wikipedia.org/wiki/Sleeping_Beauty, accessed Aug 28, 2014

[2] *A rolling stone gathers no moss*, http://en.wikipedia.org/wiki/A_rolling_stone_gathers_no_moss, accessed Aug 28, 2014

[3] Psalm 92: 13, https://www.biblegateway.com/quicksearch/?quicksearch=planted+in+the+house&qs_version=AMP, accessed Aug 28, 2014

[4] The Fruit Tree Business Growth Club, http://www.thefruittree.co.uk/how-we-work, accessed Aug 28, 2014

[5] Song of Songs 5:2-6, https://www.biblegateway.com/passage/?search=Song+of+Songs+5%3A2-6&version=AMP, accessed Aug 28, 2014

[6] John Donne, Meditation 17 Devotions upon Emergent Occasions (1623), http://en.wikisource.org/w/index.php?title=Meditation_XVII&oldid=3748254, accessed Aug 28, 2014

[7] Robert Zemeckis, *Cast Away*, movie (Dreamworks SKG: Dreamworks Distribution, 2000)

[8] Thomas Telford, http://en.wikipedia.org/wiki/Thomas_Telford, accessed July 20, 2014

Chapter 7

[1] John, C. Maxwell, *Sometimes You Win, Sometimes You Learn* (Kindle DX version) retrieved from Amazon.com, 2013

[2] T Szasz, *The Myth of Mental Illness* (50th Anniversary edition, (Kindle DX version) retrieved from Amazon.com, 2011

[3] Numbers 22:21-31, https://www.biblegateway.com/passage/?search=Numbers+22%3A21-31&version=AMP, accessed Sep 1, 2014

[4] James Dyson, https://www.youtube.com/watch?v=SWeWYGbVO7E, accessed July 25, 2014

Part 3 The Untangled Life

[1] Ephesians 2:10, https://www.biblegateway.com/quicksearch/?quicksearch=%E2%80%9CWe+are+His+workmanship%E2%80%9D&qs_version=AMP, accessed Aug 28, 2014

[2] Kary Oberbrunner, *The Deeper Path* (Baker Books: Grand Rapids, Michigan, 2013)

[3] Gill Scott, *Flow of Fruition* (Unpublished)

[4] L.P. Jacks, *Education through Recreation* (New York: Harper and Brothers, 1932) 1

Chapter 1

[1] ROGBIV, http://en.wikipedia.org/wiki/Roy_G._Biv accessed July 3, 2014

[2] David Hume, *A Brief History of the War of the Roses* (Kindle DX version) retrieved from Amazon.com, 2012

[3] Rowntrees Of York Gave Best In Value, http://en.wikipedia.org/wiki/Roy_G._Biv accessed July 3, 2014

[4] Gal 5:1, https://www.biblegateway.com/passage/?search=Gal+5%3A1&version=AMP, accessed Aug 28, 2014

[5] Danny Boyle, *Ode to England.* Comment by The New York Times columnist Sally Lyall writing the day after the *Isles of Wonder* spectacular. London Olympic Games opening ceremony. Sally Lyall, New York Times 28th July 2012.

[6] Geoffrey Himes, blogger http://blogs.citypaper.com/noise/index.php/2013/03/sxsw-danny-boyle-talks-up-new-film-trance/, accessed July 25, 2014

[7] Brene Brown, http://www.youtube.com/watch?v=iCvmsMzlF7ohttp://www.youtube.com/watch?v=iCvmsMzlF7o, accessed June 2, 2014

[8] 2 Tim 4:6, https://www.biblegateway.com/passage/?search=2 Timothy+4:6&version=AMP, accessed Aug 28, 2014

[9] Johann Wolfgang Goethe, *Colours are the deeds and suffering of light* cited by Alex Webb: Notes on The Suffering of Light - LightBox http://lightbox.time.com/2011/05/16/alex-webb-notes-on-the-suffering-of-light/#ixzz3C3qw9wyU

Chapter 2

[1] Ecclesiastes 4: 12 https://www.biblegateway.com/passage/?search
=Ecc+4%3A12&version=NIV, accessed Aug 28, 2014

[2] Grayson Perry *In the Best Possible Taste. Features The Vanity of
Small Differences* (Channel 4 UK, 2012-05-3), accessed, June 30,
2014

[3] Grayson Perry, http://en.wikipedia.org/wiki/Grayson_Perry,
accessed June 30, 2014

[4] The Rake's progress, http://smarthistory.khanacademy.org/
hogarths-a-rakes-progress.html, accessed Aug 28, 2014

[5] Bear Grylls, *The Island*, (Channel 4 UK, 2014) http://www.channel4.
com/programmes/the-island-with-bear-grylls, accessed 28, Aug 2014

[6] Maslow's Hierarchy of Needs (1943) https://www.youtube.com/
watch?v=Ugp3hm2JIqM, accessed Aug 28, 2014

[7] William Golding, *Lord of the Flies* (Kindle DX version) retrieved
from Amazon.com, 2012

[8] The Hoarder Next Door (2013) http://www.channel4.com/
programmes/the-hoarder-next-door, accessed Aug 28, 2014

[9] Zig Ziglar, http://www.ziglar.com/, accessed Aug 28, 2014

[10] Stephen R. Covey, https://www.stephencovey.com/, accessed Aug
28, 2014

[11] Tony Robbins, http://www.tonyrobbins.com/, accessed Aug 28,
2014

[12] John C. Maxwell, http://www.johnmaxwell.com/, accessed Aug 28, 2014

[13] Henry Cloud, *Necessary Endings* (Harper Collins: New York, 2010)

[14] Jackson Pollock, http://en.wikipedia.org/wiki/Drip_painting, accessed Aug 28, 2014

[15] George Eliot, *Middlemarch* (Kindle DX version) retrieved from Amazon.com, 1993

[16] Jane Austen, *Emma* (Kindle DX version) retrieved from Amazon.com, 2012

[17] Lesley Wright, *Bowel Function in Hospital Patients* https://www.rcn.org.uk/__data/assets/pdf_file/0003/235524/Series_1_Number_4.pdf, accessed Aug 9, 2014

[18] William Morris, *Hopes and Fears for Art: Five Lectures Delivered in Birmingham, London, and Nottingham, 1878 - 1881* (1882) http://en.wikiquote.org/wiki/William_Morris, accessed Aug 28, 2014

Chapter 3

[1] Gill Scott *Poem* (Unpublished)

[2] Eden, https://www.biblegateway.com/passage/?search=Genesis+2:8&version=AMP, accessed Sep 1, 2014

[3] Cherubim, https://www.biblegateway.com/passage/?dc=3&utm_expid=13466113-10.DRY5Q0U2TpaXvRe49bTgCA.3&search=Genesis+3:24&version=AMP&utm_referrer=https%3A%2F%2Fwww.biblegateway.com%2Fquicksearch%2F%3Fquicksearch%3DTree%2Bof%2Blife%26qs_version%3DAMP, accessed Aug 28, 2014

[4] Stephen R. Covey (1989) *The Seven Habits of Highly Effective People*. Simon and Schuster UK Ltd, London

[5] James Dyson, https://www.youtube.com/watch?v=SWeWYGbVO7E, accessed July 25, 2014

[6] Joe Johnston, director. *Honey I shrunk the Kids*, movie (Buena Vista Pictures,1989)

[7] Animal skin, https://www.biblegateway.com/passage/?search=Genesis+3:21&version=AMP, accessed Sep 1, 2014

[8] Law of Attraction, http://en.wikipedia.org/wiki/Law_of_attraction_(New_Thought), accessed Aug 31, 2014

[9] Joe Simpson, *Touching the Void* (Vintage: London, 2004)

[10] Watchman Nee, http://www.watchmannee.org/life-ministry.html, accessed Aug 28, 2014

[11] Eph 4:8-10, https://www.biblegateway.com/passage/?dc=3&utm_expid=13466113-10.DRY5Q0U2TpaXvRe49bTgCA.3&search=Eph+4%3A8-10&version=AMP&utm_referrer=https%3A%2F%2Fwww.biblegateway.com%2Fpassage%2F%3Fdc%3D3%26search%3DEph%2B4%253A8-10%26version%3DAMP, accessed Aug 28, 2014

[12] 2 Sam 23:5, https://www.biblegateway.com/passage/?search=2+Sam+23%3A5&version=NIV, accessed Sep 1, 2104

Final Word

[1] Rom 8: 15-21, https://www.biblegateway.com/passage/?search=Rom+8%3A+15-21&version=AMP, accessed Sep 1, 2014

[2] Flynn Rider, character quotation from *Tangled*. Directed by Nathan Greno and Byron Howard, movie after Jacob and Wilhelm Grimm's story *Rapunzel* (Walt Disney Animation Studios and Walt Disney Pictures 2010)